LABOR
AND
FOREIGN POLICY

LABOR
AND
FOREIGN POLICY

Gompers, the AFL, and the First World War, 1914-1918

SIMEON LARSON

RUTHERFORD ● MADISON ● TEANECK
Fairleigh Dickinson University Press

London: Associated University Presses

© 1975 by Associated University Presses, Inc.

Associated University Presses, Inc.
Cranbury, New Jersey 08512

Associated University Presses
108 New Bond Street
London W1Y OQX, England

Library of Congress Cataloging in Publication Data

Larson, Simeon, 1925-
　Labor and foreign policy; Gompers, the AFL, and the First World War, 1914-1918.

　Bibliography: p.
　1. Trade-unions and foreign policy—United States. 2. Gompers, Samuel, 1850-1924. 3. American Federation of Labor. 4. European War, 1914-1918—United States. 5. United States—Foreign relations—1913-1921.
I.　Title.
HD6490.F58L35　　331.88'32'0973　　73-2898
ISBN 0-8386-1290-3

PRINTED IN THE UNITED STATES OF AMERICA

For my father and my wife—two indispensable pillars of support

Contents

Preface

Trade unions and international relations have often been regarded as unrelated areas of study, each hardly able to influence the other. Yet, since 1914, organized labor has involved itself in international affairs to a degree that, at times, overshadowed its main function as a trade union. This was particularly true during the First World War, when the AFL played an important, if not essential, role in the development and implementation of Woodrow Wilson's foreign policy. The purpose of this study is to assess the effect of organized labor on this nation's foreign policy between 1914-1918, to discern the reasons for Gompers's inordinate concern with overseas policy, to note the degree to which differences arose within the Federation over Gompers's almost total acceptance of Wilson's program, and to provide guidelines for an understanding of the present role of the AFL-CIO in international affairs.

In organizing the material, a division is made between the decision-making process in foreign policy matters within the AFL and its implementation. The first two chapters revolve around the theoretical bases that underlay the Federation's position on international affairs as well as an examination of the structure of the AFL that enabled Gompers, almost single-handedly, to stamp his program on the labor movement. The remainder of the book is devoted to the role of the AFL in support of this nation's overseas program —industrially, militarily, and in the molding of public opinion. The material is concentrated on the activities of labor within the boundaries of the United States rather than on its diplomatic missions abroad or its work in the international labor movement.

9

Work on this project was begun in 1968 when the author was a graduate student at the New School for Social Research. Several members of the faculty provided this fledgling author with much-needed aid and advice. To Professors Saul K. Padover, Jacob Landynski, and Adamantia Pollis, I express my deep appreciation for their patience and understanding in giving of their time to answer my many questions. To Professor Alan Wolk of Bronx Community College, I extend my gratitude for his extremely valuable assistance and for encouraging my determination in the present work.

LABOR
AND
FOREIGN POLICY

1

The American Federation of Labor—Bases of Foreign Policy: Theory

For a century preceding the First World War, commercial rivalry, colonial expansion, and a foreign policy dedicated to the maintenance of the "balance of power" had occupied the attention of the major European powers. The results of such policies were to bear fruit in the summer of 1914, when a spark of relatively minor consequence—the assassination of Archduke Francis Ferdinand, heir to the throne of Austria-Hungary—was to ignite all of Europe and plunge the nations into a castastrophic conflict.

As the crisis deepened and each country mobilized its armed forces, a new element entered the international scene and, for a brief moment, threatened to halt the march to war. The socialist-led trade unions of Europe, ideologically grounded in the belief that the international ties of the workingmen were stronger than their allegiance to the country of their birth, and committed to a policy to enforce the peace, gathered to consider their response to the call of their respective governments for money, arms, and men—the necessary implements of war. It was to be the supreme test between international working class solidarity and the appeal of nationalist sentiment to defend the honor and sanctity of the homeland. The contest was short-lived and decisive. Nationalism emerged triumphant and with a new-born self-confidence easily crushed the theoretical assumptions that had nurtured internationalism. It was not until 1917, with the triumph of the Russian Bolsheviks, that a new internationalism would rise on the fallen structures and challenge anew the supremacy of nationalism.

If the demise of internationalism was to have a profound effect on European trade unionism, its theoretical impact on the leadership of the American Federation of Labor was slight. This was not surprising, since the sum and substance of trade-union theory as advocated by the AFL—class collaborationism, pragmatism, and opportunism—militated against any concept that would bring organized workers of America into irreconcilable conflict with the owners of industry or leaders of the government. What the war did accomplish was to reinforce an ideology already embraced by the AFL, and to wed its leaders more firmly to the belief that support of American foreign policy was to be equated with patriotism and loyalty to America's ideals as expressed in its institutions.

As a result, the European conflict did not lead the Federation into a reexamination of its trade-union philosophy, but simply opened up before it, in the realm of foreign affairs, a new area of participation. The Federation saw its role in international affairs as a means of accomplishing some of the objectives it had so valiantly striven for since its inception. As such, during the First World War, it did not seek to innovate or create policy in foreign relations, but was more than willing to become an instrument in the hands of the Wilson Administration in the hope that its services would be amply rewarded. Essentially, it followed a program of pragmatism and opportunism.

The theoretical factors underlying the making of foreign-policy decisions within the American Federation of Labor were a direct outgrowth of its domestic philosophy. Each complemented and supported the other; each was a projection of the other. So integrated were the two that a brief explanation of how the Federation conceived of its role seems imperative.

To Samuel Gompers, president of the AFL for every year except

1895, action and achievement were far superior to abstract reasoning and theory. He conceived of organized labor not as a theory but as a living reality, whose existence depended on practical men concerned with immediate gain rather than with "chimerical tomorrows." Success, to the AFL leadership, became the standard upon which all things were judged.[1]

Since its inception, the Federation favored the thesis that the economic power of the workers, as exercised through their trade unions, was the fundamental power and that whatever influence they might gain in national and international affairs was derivative, and in direct proportion to the development of their economic organizations. Since gains won through collective bargaining were regarded as permanent, while advantages obtained through legislation were temporary, the workers were urged to concentrate on strengthening their trade unions and not to divert their energies into political channels. Thus the main thrust of AFL activity was along economic, not legislative lines.

Gompers was determined to avoid the example of the European trade unions, where no recognized boundary line was established between the economic organizations of the workers and the political Socialist Party. In order to be practical and effective, Gompers favored nonpartisan political tactics.

Gompers saw in the American experience, in the unending struggle of the people to develop and maintain democratic institutions, a refutation of socialist theory. He was enamored with the concept of rugged individualism, and held that the trade-union movement, as well as the policies of government, should be directed along voluntary lines. Choice was an individual act and each worker, as well as each national union, should be free to pursue the policy it desired. The Federation had no power of coercion over any of its constituent parts. It could only recommend; it could not command. Such was the creed of voluntarism.

Gompers had a Jeffersonian fear of the growing power and author-

---

1. Samuel Gompers, *Seventy Years of Life and Labor* (New York: E. P. Dutton and Company, 1925), 1: 403, 424. Gompers frequently castigated his opponents as men who failed to achieve concrete results, or, in the case of Eugene Victor Debs, as a leader of "lost causes."

ity of the state. In language reminiscent of our third president, he held that "there never was a government in the history of the world and there is not one today that when a critical moment came, did not exercise tyranny over the people." He was a firm believer in the less government the better and carried out this policy to such an extent that he opposed legislative action curbing the trusts or establishing the eight-hour day for nongovernment employees. The AFL, along with the National Association of Manufacturers and the National Civic Federation, was to become a firm proponent of "laissez-faire."

The key to our understanding of the Federation's domestic and foreign policies lies in its attitude toward the social structure within which it functioned. The leaders of the Federation early came to the conclusion that it was their duty "not to work for the downfall or the destruction" of American capitalism, but to work for "its fuller development and evolution." It saw the ideal economic system as one in which organized labor and industry had entered into a partnership on equal terms in which each acknowledged the needs of the other, and engaged in collective bargaining as equals.

As early as 1883, in testimony before a United States Senate Committee, Gompers argued that a well-organized trade-union movement was a check upon the more radical elements in society.[2] He offered the conservative leadership of the American Federation of Labor, with its craft-union structure, as a bulwark against the dangerous maximalists as exemplified by the Industrial Workers of the World.[3] It was Gompers's hope that the rising strength of Socialism, and later Boshevism, would force the major industrialists to unite with the AFL by a process of mutual concessions and agreements.[4] He was firmly convinced that had there been a bona-fide labor movement in Russia the Bolsheviks would never have

2. Testimony before a United States Senate Committee upon the Relations Between Capital and Labor, August 18, 1883, in Samuel Gompers, *Labor and the Common Welfare* (New York: E. P. Dutton and Company, 1919), p. 175.
3. Frank T. Carlton, "The Changing A.F.L.," *The Survey* (November 21, 1914), pp. 191-93. The author ends with a plea to employers to stop fighting the AFL or else force it to adopt more radical tactics like the IWW.
4. Ralph M. Easley to Gompers, June 21, 1915, National Civic Federation Manuscripts, Manuscript Division, New York Public Library, New York City; Gompers to Easley, June 23, 1915, *ibid.*

come to power; or, conversely, the AFL would have saved America from a similar fate.[5]

Rejecting any blueprint or standard of labor's ultimate goals or objectives and espousing a policy of "pure and simple trade unionism," the AFL failed to develop any comprehensive set of ideas concerning foreign affairs. It was content to go along from day to day, in a practical manner, reacting to events as they occurred on the international scene. This is not to indicate that the Federation failed to formulate any policy emanating out of the needs of the workers, such as international peace and disarmament. What it does signify is that the AFL's policies on international affairs were often vague and general in nature and, not being anchored in a concrete philosophy, were subject to wide variations as dictated by the pragmatic needs of the Federation. This becomes particularly evident during the European War of 1914-18.

Prior to World War I, the AFL had voiced its unwavering devotion to international peace and disarmament. Gompers was a firm opponent of the use of force as a means of settling disputes between nations. He favored international arbitration as the best instrument for preventing differences in the international community from being resolved by armed conflict. When the United States Senate in 1897 was considering ratifying an arbitration treaty between the United States and Great Britain, Gompers campaigned in its behalf. He was a vice-president of the National Peace Congresses held in 1907 and 1909, which had as its main purpose the abolishment of war as an instrument to enforce a nation's foreign policy. Similarly, Gompers enthusiastically supported the recommendations of Winston Churchill in 1913 for a naval holiday in which the governments of the signatory nations agreed to refrain from engaging in naval rearmament.

Interwoven with Gompers's plaintive appeals to the leaders of all nations in behalf of world peace and disarmament was a decidedly militant if not threatening tone. In 1899, Gompers was advocating the intervention by workers in international affairs if those in author-

---

5. Address at the Convention of the National Lecturer's Association, April 11, 1918, in Samuel Gompers, *American Labor and the War* (New York: George H. Doran Co., 1919), p. 195; Address under the auspices of Central Labor Union, Boston, May 1, 1918, in Samuel Gompers, *Common Welfare*, p. 267.

ity failed to settle their disputes by peaceful means. ". . .I look forward to the time," Gompers stated, "when the workers will settle this question—by the dock workers refusing to handle goods that are to be used to destroy their fellow man, and by the seamen of the world united in one organization . . . absolutely refusing to strike down their fellow man."[6] At the 1907 convention of the AFL, Gompers warned the governments of the world that the masses had it in their power to unleash a mighty force for peace if any statesman sought to thwart their desires.[7] The fraternization of the workers of the world in an international labor movement, he declared, would be an almost irresistible force for peace.[8]

Yet, the professed internationalism and militancy of the AFL leaders was to be tempered by nationalist considerations. The workingman, Gompers proclaimed, would always answer the call of patriotism and fight for his country. It was not military service that Gompers found objectionable but rather the manner in which men were inducted into the armed forces. If based on voluntary principles, the AFL offered no objection to workers' serving as citizen soldiers. It was only the European system of "obligatory service" that Gompers found repugnant.[9] Since organized labor had an obligation to fight for its membership, then nations, Gompers maintained, had the same obligation to fight for the rights of its citizens.[10] Self-proclaimed pacifist that he was, the AFL president was not a proponent of unilateral disarmament. In reality, Gompers's pacifism was to prove more rhetorical than actual, and would gradually dissipate itself when faced with concrete situations and not just abstractions.

The movement of the AFL away from internationalism and pacifism and toward nationalism and militancy was further evidenced

6. Quoted in Address Before the Sixteenth Annual Meeting of the National Civic Federation, January 18, 1916, in Gompers, *American Labor and the War*, pp. 51-52.
7. Annual Report before the 1907 AFL convention, in Gompers, *Common Welfare*, pp. 219-20. Gompers stigmatized those who disturbed peace as being motivated by a "sordid purpose." War, he continued, retards progress and civilization and has a detrimental effect on mankind long after actual hostilities are terminated.
8. Annual Report before the 1904 AFL Convention, *ibid.*, p. 226.
9. *American Federationist* 17 (March 1910): 222-24.
10. Proceedings of the National Arbitration and Peace Congress (New York, 1907), p. 251, cited by Delber Lee McKee, *The American Federation of Labor and American Foreign Policy, 1886-1912*, Ph.D. dissertation, Stanford University, 1952.

in 1914. When "Wild Bill" Haywood, chief organizer of the IWW, told an audience that in the event Congress declared war on Mexico, the workers would automatically start the "greatest general strike this country had ever seen," James M. Duncan, president of the International Typographical Union, vociferously disagreed.[11] Proclaiming that he was "first of all an American," Duncan declared that he was "for America in any struggle in which its honor is involved." The speech served to split the labor movement in Indiana.[12] Yet, the unbridled nationalism of the president of the International Typographical Union was to be followed with almost Pavlovian regularity by the leading figures of the Federation during the war. However, as in Indiana, any international policy designed to involve the United States in a foreign war was to encounter rising opposition among many of the national unions, and particularly among the rank and file.

If in 1899, 1904, and 1907 Gompers had advocated a general strike in behalf of peace, he slowly began to retreat from this position as the reality of the world crisis became more apparent. In April 1914, barely six months before the outbreak of hostilities, the *American Federationist*, official organ of the American Federation of Labor, began publishing articles decrying the use of a general strike to obtain peace as ineffective and perhaps incurring a vast amount of social suffering and industrial calamity. In its stead, the article stressed more studies on the effects of armaments, the democratization of diplomacy, and the elimination of passion and prejudice among peoples and nations.[13] Thus, prior to the outbreak of war, Gompers had already begun to decry any direct movement or activity on the part of workingmen or their trade unions to influence their respective governments on the crucial issue of war or peace. As a suitable alternative, he offered the weapon of education, the implementation of which would rest very lightly on the labor movement.

It should be noted at this point that prior to the commencement of hostilities in Europe, a variety of opinions concerning the role of labor in international affairs existed among Gompers's inner circle.

11. *New York Times*, April 20, 1914, p. 1.
12. *Ibid.*, April 21, 1914, p. 4.
13. B. N. Langdon-Davies, "Militarism and Labor," *American Federationist* 21 (April 1914): 303-6.

For example, in a speech before the Massachusetts Peace Society in May, James Duncan (not to be confused with James M. Duncan of the Typographical Union), first vice-president of the AFL, and one of Gompers's closest associates, was still advocating overt collective action by labor to halt capitalistic intrigue that led to war.[14] However, as the war began, Gompers was gradually able to unite this group into a solid phalanx in support of his foreign policies.

The onset of war in the summer of 1914 publicly shook Gompers loose from his pacifist moorings. The Carnegie Peace Foundation had offered to publish all his articles and addresses on international peace. When war broke out Gompers stated that he immediately hastened to the Foundation and withdrew his manuscript.[15] He was no longer a pacifist. Gompers held that his conversion from pacifism was an act of pragmatism and an acceptance of reality. When the workers of the world rallied to the colors at the request of kaiser and czar, president and king, Gompers decided that he had been living in a "fool's paradise," and that his own conception of the impossibility of war was based on personal desire and not on objective reality.[16] Henceforth, relying on his new understanding of the world, he would call upon the nation to take steps to defend itself.[17]

In abandoning pacifism, Gompers sought to lay the groundwork for a labor foreign policy whose main ideological pillars of support would be a rampant nationalism, a belief that "America is the apotheosis of all that is right," and boundless faith in the Wilson Administration.[18]

The war quickly demonstrated to the AFL the inadequacy of the theory of internationalism. Gompers saw its failure rooted in a misunderstanding of human nature. Man, he proclaimed, was governed more by instinct and impulse than by reason and reflection. Patriotism, to Gompers, was a "strong compelling force—a primal in-

14. AFL, *Weekly News Letter* (May 30, 1914).
15. Gompers, *Seventy Years,* 2: 331.
16. Address before Wilson Eight-Hour League, October 13, 1916, in Gompers, *Common Welfare*, p. 230; AFL, *Proceedings* (1915), pp. 386-88.
17. Address at annual meeting of National Civic Federation, January 18, 1916, in Gompers, *Common Welfare*, pp. 228-29.
18. Speech under the auspices of American Alliance for Labor and Democracy, November 8, 1918, in Gompers, *American Labor and the War*, p. 268; Gompers, *Seventy Years,* 1: 551; *ibid.,* 2: 545-46.

stinct in the individual."[19] It was proof positive that the ties that bound the workingman to the nation were stronger than the ties that bound him to his fellows. The Federation leaders viewed nationalism as overcoming the class interests of the workers.[20] Henceforth they would maintain that to be an effective internationalist one had first to embrace nationalism.[21]

Gompers's initial interpretation of the war was in marked contrast to his later views. With the firing of the first shots and the realization that the conflict had begun, Gompers immediately castigated the war as "unnatural, unjustified and unholy" and "condemnable from every viewpoint."[22] He condemned the Austrian declaration of war on Serbia as an act "for the glory and aggrandizement of an effete royalty."[23] To Gompers, the war had but one aim: to divert the attention of people from their domestic problems and to demoralize organized labor so that it would no longer be a threat to the entrenched dynasties. Agreeing with the Central Federated Union of New York, the leaders of the AFL regarded the outbreak of hostilities as a gigantic conspiracy directed against the growing demand of working men and women for a better life.[24] During the first few months of the war, a remarkable unanimity of opinion existed among the Federation heads, the leaders of the national and international unions, and the rank and file. All opposed the war with equal fervor.[25] However, the honeymoon was to be of short duration. The history of Federation policy on war and peace during the First World War is a record of unceasing dissension among the various elements composing the American Federation of Labor.

Writing in September, Gompers was still persuaded that the outbreak of war was a tactical victory for the ruling classes of Europe

19. From article in *Harpers Weekly* (March 10, 1915), in Gompers, *Common Welfare*, pp. 214-15.
20. *Ibid.;* Gompers, *Seventy Years,* 2: 389-90.
21. *Ibid.,* 2: 405.
22. Gompers to *Chicago Examiner,* August 7, 1914, Gompers Manuscripts, Manuscript Division, Library of Congress, Washington, D.C.
23. *Railway Carmen's Journal* 19 (September 1914): 543.
24. *Ibid.,* 543; *American Federationist* 21 (September 1914): 734; *The Carpenters* 33 (September 1914): 13.
25. Examples of the unity of opinion at the time may be seen in the following two journals, which were often critical of Gompers's positions on international affairs. *Coast Seamen's Journal* (August 26, 1914); *The Tailor* (September 1, 1914).

and "had there been only ordinary time . . . this war could have been averted by the influence, power and determination of the workers."[26] The AFL leadership stated its willingness to lead any movement in behalf of a negotiated peace—a position it was later to oppose vehemently.[27]

Gompers cast about for means to end the war, but the trade-union philosophy of the AFL served to narrow his options. His creed of voluntarism militated against the use of United States economic power to coerce the nations of Europe, and his concept of "pure and simple" trade unionism did not lead itself to collective, direct action by labor in behalf of peace. Gompers was content to issue declarations, and have the executive council of the AFL pass resolutions.[28] There is no evidence that the president of the AFL engaged in any organizational effort or participated in any collective activity that would have brought meaningful pressure to bear on either the United States or any of the European nations to take steps to halt the conflict. On the contrary, as will be indicated later, a question arises as to whether a discrepancy existed between Gompers's stated positions and the policies he pursued behind the scenes.

Gompers's analysis of the war tended to localize responsibility for the conflict. Autocracy, in the form of the Kaiser, czar, and king, he maintained, must bear the main responsibility for the on-rushing conflict. Therefore, if, as he reasoned, it was the misrule of a handful of unprincipled autocrats, masters in their own lands, that had been one of the primary causes of the war, it followed that democratic changes in some of the European governments might ensure a future of peace and guarantee a better life for the working masses. His aims and objectives were of a limited nature. He did not regard the war as determined by economic forces, but rather as the result of German autocracy and militarism. Neither did he see any connection, however remote, between industrial interests in the United States and the war in Europe.

As one traveled further away from AFL headquarters in Washing-

26. Gompers to Ralph M. Easley, September 5, 1914, NCF MSS.
27. Gompers to Executive Council, September 5, 1914, Gompers MSS; *American Federationist* 21 (October 1914): 868-69.
28. Gompers to Matthew Woll, August 14, 1914, Gompers MSS.

ton and moved closer to the local labor centers, the criticism of the origins of the war became more incisive and fundamental, and provided the theoretical basis for an activist approach by the rank and file. Their interpretation of the war was largely grounded in the doctrine of economic determinism and, unlike the AFL leaders, they did not exclude United States industrial corporations from a share of the responsibility nor did they exclude the possibility of future American participation in the conflict. The war, in their opinion, had an economic base and was a joint venture of American as well as European capitalism.[29] They foresaw an effort by American capitalists to plunge the American working class into the war in order to expand their business and power.[30] To thwart such a development, they mounted a dual attack. On the one hand, they sought to eliminate the economic advantages to be gained through war by demanding the nationalization of all industries manufacturing arms and munitions, and government acquisition of all patent rights for war equipment;[31] and, on the other, by militantly utilizing the economic and political power of the trade unions in behalf of peace.

While an economic interpretation of the war was readily acceptable to an overwhelming number of trade union leaders and their membership—the 1914 convention of the AFL having unanimously adopted such a proposal with the passive acquiescence of the Gompers group[32]—the suggestion that the AFL use direct action against war was nimbly sidetracked by Gompers.[33] But the agitation for a more specific response by labor in behalf of peace continued unabated. Typical of this line of thinking was the labor *Bulletin* of San Francisco. Praising the anti-war position of the AFL adopted at the Philadelphia convention, it declared that "if the AFL stands fast

29. *The Tailor* (September 1, 1914).
30. *The American Flint* 6 (December 1914): 1-2.
31. AFL *Proceedings* (1914), pp. 467-68.
32. *Ibid.*
33. *American Federationist* 21 (October 1914): 855. In July 1914, prior to the war, the Central Labor Union requested the Executive Council to issue an appeal to all union labor to refrain from enlisting in the armed forces as a protest against war. Gompers did not accept this suggestion, but neither did he refute it. His tactic was to imply that the leadership knew best how to work for peace and was following a course that it deemed correct. In this manner, he avoided any direct confrontation with the membership or trade-union leaders on issues that were popular with them.

against war, and against all public policies which lead to war . . . the peace of the United States will be as safe as men can make it. Without the consent of the 2,000,000 members of the AFL, the United States can never make war.''[34]

The words of the *Bulletin* were gradually to grow into a major irritant to the Federation leaders. Such an activist program was not only contrary to their conception of the role of a trade union, but it jeopardized their grand design of amity between capital and labor by its implication that the United States Government contemplated entering the war for other than honorable reasons—a concept totally alien to their way of thinking. The differences between the two positions slowly began to sharpen and emerge.

In his Labor Day address on September 7, Gompers added a discordant note to the general outward harmony that prevailed among labor concerning the European conflict. While condemning the war as one of "aggrandizement and conquest," he saw something positive developing from it—international labor solidarity, international law, a system of arbitration, and a code of international morality as a standard for the maintenance of peace.[35] Gompers thus added a new dimension to the debate. He sought to weigh the effects of the war on the proverbial scales of justice, balancing both good and evil. The AFL president, at this time, obviously regarded the negative aspects of the war as outweighing any positive results, but the impact of the statement became clear: the European War, no matter how indirectly, would yet serve as an instrument to advance civilization and mankind. This was in sharp contrast to the overwhelming majority of labor men who, until the United States entered the war, pictured the conflict as an unmitigated evil with no saving features.[36] However, Gompers was to become so enamored with this idea, and so to build upon it, that in a few short years he was to label the war "the most

---

34. Quoted in AFL, *Weekly News Letter,* November 28, 1914.
35. Speech on Labor Day, September 7, 1914, in Gompers, *American Labor and the War,* pp. 20-21.
36. The membership of the American Federation of Labor, composed of diverse national groups, maintained a steady and unremitting opposition to the war. This was particularly true of the Irish, German, and Jewish trade unionists who fought against any aid to the Allies or United States participation in the conflict.

wonderful crusade ever entered upon by men in the whole history of the world."[37]

To emphasize further his distaste for the theory of economic determinism as a primary causative factor in the war, Gompers laid greater stress on the role of human nature. In his Labor Day speech, he began to touch on some of the ideas once proposed by the philosopher William James.[38] He alluded to the war as being instinctively alluring to man. He spoke in fascination of the "whirl and thrill" of it all, of its "compelling magnetism," of the wonderful patriotic emotions it engenders, and of the bravery that "goes straight to the heart."[39]

The acceptance by Gompers of the European War as being partly rooted in human nature further accelerated his movement away from pacifism, and added momentum to his eventual rise as one of the foremost proponents of preparedness for national defense, and of America's entry into the conflict on the side of the Allies. As the initial shock of the war diminished, the primary question to occupy the attention of organized labor was the role of the United States in relation to the war. The debate focused around two central issues: national defense, and the nature of true neutrality. In each instance, Gompers was to move further away from past labor positions on peace and disarmament and in the direction of supporting, in its entirety, the foreign policies of Woodrow Wilson.

As the war progressed and its effect on America became more pronounced, Gompers increasingly identified the Federation's "war policy" with that of the Wilson Administration. The reason lies partly in Gompers's pragmatic outlook. He states in his Autobiography that he had foreseen before other labor leaders the impact of the European struggle upon United States labor and that, above and beyond any other issue, organized labor would be judged by its activity in this area.[40] The overriding issue for the president of the AFL

37. Address before Canadian House of Commons, April 26, 1918, in Gompers, *American Labor and the War*, p. 197.
38. I find no evidence indicating that Gompers read, or was influenced by William James.
39. Speech on Labor Day at Plattsburg, N. Y., September 7, 1914, Gompers, *American Labor and the War*, pp. 17-18.
40. Gompers, *Seventy Years*, 2: 346.

was to be judged "right." This meant unquestioning support of the Allies and the government. To this end, Gompers willingly surrendered some of the basic theoretical tenets that were the foundation of his labor policies. His concept of "more, more" for the workers was sacrificed to the expediency of a war economy; his creed of voluntarism, which he believed to be at the heart of free man's relationship to his trade union and government, was cruelly ignored; and his belief that government should not interfere in labor-management relations was all but forgotten. All this, according to Gompers, was done in the name of patriotism and practicality. But to many others it was regarded as "cynical opportunism."[41]

The efforts of the peace societies to resolve the international conflict were early opposed by Gompers as impractical and impotent.[42] Besides, he felt they placed too high a value on peace. In his thinking, peace was not the ultimate goal. "More abhorrent than war," the Federation leader would proclaim, "was to be robbed of the birthright of freedom, justice, safety and character."[43]

The logic of Gompers's thinking eventually led him into opposing any peaceful settlement of the war that did not first resolve the moral issues involved. Since he viewed the German government as inherently immoral and sought as a primary condition for the cessation of hostilities the removal of that government from office—a prospect he knew full well could not be accomplished without a German surrender—his position led him to become one of the leading exponents of a victor's peace.[44]

This becomes clearly evident, as early as 1914, by the stand of the AFL at its annual convention. Andrew Furuseth, president of the Seamen's International Union, proposed that since no government or

---

41. Gompers to the Editor of *The Public,* April 3, 1918, Gompers MSS.
42. AFL, *Proceedings* (1914), pp. 48-49.

43. Gompers to William J. Mahoney of Washington Peace Committee of 100, June 23, 1915, Gompers MSS; Gompers to Ernest Bohm, June 18, 1915, Woodrow Wilson Manuscripts, Manuscript Division, Library of Congress, Washington, D.C.
44. Address before the Convention of the League to Enforce Peace, May 26, 1916, in Gompers, *American Labor and the War,* pp. 79-80. Gompers flatly states that "if I could stop the war now by a turn of my hand, I would not do so."

people could be blamed for the war, the people of the United States "judge none of those who are engaged in this war but to tender to them our profound sympathy."[45] The Committee on International Relations, of which Gompers was a member, voted nonconcurrence on the grounds it was against any peace that did not resolve basic wrongs such as the suppression of national aspirations in the Balkans.[46] Since neither of the belligerents, at that historical moment, could militarily impose their will on the other, the AFL in effect opted for a continuation of war. After the United States entered the conflict, Gompers often boasted of the fact that he had approved of our entrance much earlier, but yielded to the judgment of the president.[47] If he originally had viewed the war as "unholy and unjustified," its character, in his mind, was to change radically when America became a participant. It now became the "greatest event in human history since the creation."[48] As millions of men were slaughtered, the leaders of the Federation saw the war as "doing more to humanize the world than anything else in history."[49]

When the United States entered the war, Gompers took the unqualified position that the primary task of labor was to win the war and, until this was accomplished, labor would, as far as possible, not press the government for an adjustment of its grievances.[50] The AFL was the only trade-union movement that took such a position. In most European countries, the trade unions were of the opinion that they first had to settle their grievances with the government before they could give it full support. Labor's cooperation and self-identification with the Administration had, by 1918, reached such a stage that some would regard the AFL as having "ceased to function

45. AFL, *Proceedings* (1914), pp. 473-74.
46. *Ibid.*
47. Speech at a meeting under the auspices of the National Security League, September 14, 1917, in Gompers, *American Labor and the War*, p. 121.
48. *Ibid.*, pp. 132, 150, 166, 173, 179. This theme runs continuously throughout many of Gompers's speeches during the wartime period.
49. *New York Times,* June 7, 1918, p. 11.
50. Notes of a lecture by John P. Frey at Harvard Student Seminar, May 12, 1948, John P. Frey Manuscripts, Manuscript Division, Library of Congress, Washington, D.C.

as an independent body."[51] The leaders of the Federation did not regard such a state of affairs as unfortunate but rather saw it as emanating from their general conception of the role of trade unions in the American capitalistic society.

The world crisis, to Gompers, opened up a new era for the labor movement. The Administration's concern for organized labor became apparent in the light of the experiences of organized labor in England and France. The failure of the British government to reach an early accord with labor had, for a time, paralyzed the British munitions industry, while in France the same attitude toward labor had brought the French army to the verge of mutiny. Gompers did not intend to follow the example of European labor. Governed by pragmatic rules that established success as the highest standard, Gompers created his own general law, which he believed would meet the needs of the situation. The measure of labor's progress, reasoned the AFL leader, was in direct ratio to the degree of its support of the government in its "war program."[52] If labor cooperated, Gompers felt certain it could secure government recognition and vastly increase its power.[53] The AFL envisioned itself as being accepted into the inner circles of government and sharing coequal power with other interests in policy formulation. It predicated labor's gains on the good will of the Wilson Administration rather than on its own strength and power.

Wilson's consideration for the support of the AFL was providing labor an influence in Washington far beyond the proportion of its membership.[54] Bemused by their own wishful thinking, the leaders of the AFL saw a new role for labor in the world of international affairs and even envisioned its president, Samuel Gompers, as a member of the American delegation to the Peace Conference.[55] The

51. George P. West, "The Progress of American Labor," *The Nation* (June 29, 1918), pp. 753-55. The article justifies Gompers's alliance with the Federal Government on the basis of the record gains labor achieved during the war. However, the author also laments the fact that labor sacrificed all of its early idealism for the sake of being practical.
52. *Coast Seamen's Journal*, March 21, 1917.
53. *Ibid.;* Gompers to John A. Flett, February 25, 1918, Gompers MSS.
54. *The New Republic* (March 10, 1917), pp. 157-58.
55. *The Boilermakers' Journal* 30 (October 1918): 737-38; Executive Council to Saint Paul Convention, *American Federationist* 25 (July 1918): 577-84. At its 1916 convention, the AFL proposed that world labor prevail upon their respective governments to grant labor representation in the national delegations each would send to the World Peace Congress. This demand, the AFL held, would be in accordance with fundamental democratic procedure of granting labor representation on that body which would be all important in determining the structure of the postwar world.

growing world power of the United States raised labor's hopes that its influence overseas, particularly in international labor matters, would grow in proportion to the increasing strength of the United States in world affairs.[56] Curiously, the Federation found common ground with the great financial interests of the country led by the House of Morgan. Financial assistance to the Allies was heartily applauded by the AFL because it regarded such assistance as increasing American influence in the debtor nations. Similarly, it saw the influence of the American labor movement as "vastly extended through the making of this war loan."[57] In effect, labor viewed itself not only as the beneficiary, but as a partner in America's emergence as a world power.

Gompers's support of the Wilson Administration also had another key objective—the enhancement of his own position within the AFL and the destruction of dual unions outside the Federation that challenged its principle of craft unionism.

Until the entrance of the United States into the war, socialist opposition to Gompers was strong. In the 1912 Convention, the socialist candidate for the presidency of the AFL, Max J. Hayes, polled 5,073 votes to Gompers's 11,974.[58] The acceleration of socialist power within the national unions continued at a rapid pace until the outbreak of the war. The socialists' position on the war made them the object of continual harassment, and coupled with their internal dissension, they soon declined as a significant force within the Federation.[59] Gompers effectively used the war hysteria to brand them as traitors to their country and agents of the Kaiser.[60]

Gompers's support of Wilson's "war aims" and the Administration's identification with the AFL's labor philosophy led both into an alliance to crush radical labor groups such as the IWW. Bill Haywood later claimed that the move by the Department of Justice to crush the IWW was inspired by Gompers.[61] The AFL president urged Secretary of War Baker to crush it because of its "arrog-

---

56. *Coast Seamen's Journal* (October 17, 1917).
57. *Ibid.*
58. AFL, *Proceedings* (1912), 354-55.
59. David J. Saposs, *Left Wing Unionism* (New York: International Publishers, 1926), pp. 36-39.
60. Gompers, *American Labor and the War*, pp. 97, 146, 262-63; idem, *Common Welfare*, p. 263.
61. William D. Haywood, *Bill Haywood's Book* (New York: International Publishers, 1929), p. 299.

ant disregard of constitutional and common law.''[62] The plan to decimate the IWW, involving as it did the Council of National Defense, on whose Advisory Commission Samuel Gompers served, was unlikely to have evolved without the active acknowledgement and support of the Federation president.[63]

At the time of Wilson's election in 1912, some of the basic ideology of the Federation was under severe attack. This was particularly true in the area of political activity where the nonpartisan "reward your friends and punish your enemies" philosophy had achieved little in the way of concrete results. In 1906, Gompers had been forced to acknowledge that labor's efforts to secure legislation favorable to its cause or to prevent the enactment of unfavorable legislation had been a dismal failure. Seeking to improve labor's effectiveness in its dealings with the Executive and Legislative branches of government, Gompers had called a conference of the heads of all national and international unions to consider labor's political role. The conference formulated a document, known as labor's Bill of Grievances, which was to be presented to President Theodore Roosevelt, the Senate, and the Speaker of the House. In its Bill of Grievances, the AFL complained of government inaction in passing an anti-injunction bill, in failing to provide for an effective eight-hour law for all federal workers, in protecting the workingman from the competition of convict labor, in restricting immigration, in instituting additional safety procedures for seamen, and in making the anti-trust laws more effective against monopolies. The petition of the AFL for legislative relief found little sympathy in the halls of Congress or at the White House. Gompers admitted that unless some practical legislative gains could be demonstrated, he would be forced to abandon this policy.[64]

The inauguration of Woodrow Wilson as president of the United States was to salvage for Gompers some of his cardinal principles and strengthen his position as leader of organized labor. At Wilson's

62. Charles A. Madison, *American Labor Leaders* (New York: Frederick Ungar Publishing Company, 1950), p. 87.
63. Felix Frankfurter to Secretary of War Baker, Memorandum of September 4, 1917, Baker Manuscripts, Manuscript Division, Library of Congress, Washington, D.C.; H.C. Peterson and Gilbert C. Fite, *Opponents of War* (Madison: University of Wisconsin Press, 1957), p. 62; William Preston Jr., *Aliens and Dissenters* (Cambridge: Harvard University Press, 1963), p. 129.
64. Gompers, *Seventy Years,* 2: 275-76, 294.

behest, the Sixty-third Congress enacted many items in labor's Bill of Grievances. Chief among these was the Clayton Act, which Gompers regarded as labor's "Magna Carta."[65] This enabled the president of the AFL to boast of the effectiveness of the nonpartisan political approach.

One of Gompers's most pressing problems was to obtain and consolidate rank-and-file support for the war. Of immediate concern was the amelioration of industrial grievances. The Administration heartily cooperated in meeting some of the most pressing needs of the workers, although the record number of strikes during the war testified to its only modest success.

But in the eyes of millions of American workers the war could be justified only if it were truly a war to make the world "safe for democracy." President Wilson's rhetoric certainly created such an impression. Gompers followed suit, making use of such vague generalizations as a war for "justice, freedom and democracy."[66] When it came to more clearly defining the Federation's postwar reconstruction program, Gompers was reluctant. He saw labor's main goal as the winning of the war and hesitated to raise subjects that would test the unity and solidarity of labor and perhaps cause divisiveness.[67] A request for such a program by a pro-war socialist was succinctly answered by Gompers: "Ought we to have our minds diverted from the will to fight and win for freedom?"[68]

At the 1918 Convention, Gompers refused to articulate any concrete demands in regard to war aims or to establish a fundamental program to be placed before the Peace Congress. He would not attempt to hinder the effectiveness of the work of the American delegation by an effort, prior to the Peace Conference, to apply "fundamental principles to concrete problems."[69] Again, at a time when it had the strength to demand concessions for its postwar aims, the Federation abdicated its responsibility. As a result, the AFL lagged far behind the European trade unions in establishing a reconstruction

65. Gompers, *American Labor and the War*, pp. 195-96.
66. Gompers to A. Greenstein, July 1, 1918, Gompers MSS.
67. *American Federationist* 25 (October 1918): 915-16; Gompers to John Spargo, March 22, 1918, Gompers MSS.
68. *Ibid.*
69. AFL, *Proceedings* (1918), p. 54.

program at the end of the war. The effect was to give President Wilson wider leverage in formulating his own position at the Conference. At the same time, it diminished labor's future impact on domestic and foreign affairs, since the need for AFL cooperation in the postwar period would be minimal in comparison to the great need for labor's cooperation during the war.

Thus labor emerged as one of the strongest supporters of the foreign policy of the Wilson Administration. So intimate did its relationship become as to earn for it the sobriquet of being just another branch of the government. Pragmatic to the core, the leadership of the AFL viewed the rise of the United States as a world power and, as a consequence, the heightened importance of foreign-policy formulation, as an instrument to advance the interests of the Federation as well as to entrench their own power within that organization.

Convinced of its own limitations and placing little reliance on its ability successfully to organize large masses of American workers in the face of employers' hostility, the Federation sought to reach an accommodation with those elements in society most antagonistic to it. It saw the war as a common enterprise on behalf of all the American people and hoped that support of the Administration's foreign policies would enable it to obtain recognition from both government and industry. To the Federation leadership, this was a "statesmanlike" approach. Gompers's philosophy exerted an important influence on labor. The position of the AFL-CIO today on American foreign policy may be said to have its roots in the years between 1914 and 1918.

2

The American Federation of Labor—Bases of Foreign Policy: Structure

Foreign policy ideas in the American Federation of Labor were largely the private creation of the president of that organization although, constitutionally, no such power had been vested in the office. That Samuel Gompers was able to monopolize this function during the First World War was due more to the aggressive and charismatic personality of the man than to any other factor. Utilizing the emergency and its attendant pressures to conform, Gompers was able to stamp his foreign policies on organized labor even though, at times, considerable opposition developed to some of his programs. This chapter briefly attempts to analyze how the office of the president of the AFL, bereft of constitutional power and enforcement instrumentalities, was able to transform itself into the guiding hand that led the Federation, despite a background of anti-militarism and pacifism, into unquestioned support of Wilson's war policies.

The American Federation of Labor was not, and is not today, an organization where power is centralized, but a federation composed of autonomous unions, united by broadly interpreted rules and confronting similar problems, each possessing complete independence within its own sphere of operation.[1] Its foundation was anchored on the twin pillars of craft unionism and trade autonomy. The function of the Federation was to settle jurisdictional disputes, influence public opinion, encourage the sale of union-made goods, systematize legislative lobbying, provide a source of strength in strikes, aid in organizing the unorganized, and generally to coordinate the activities of the national and international unions.[2]

The supreme law of the American Federation of Labor is a constitution. Final authority is vested in a convention, which meets annually. Carrying out the mandates of the convention are the elected officials and an Executive Council.

Proud of their philosophy of voluntarism, these officials often boasted of their lack of power. In testimony before the House Lobby Investigation Committee, they confidently described their duties as being to advise, suggest, and recommend. As if to emphasize this point, they often proclaimed that they could "not command one man in all American to do anything." Authority rested in the national and international unions, which could, and did, defy the decisions of the president, executive council, and convention.[3]

While the provisions of the constitution did not delegate vast powers to the office of the president, neither did they burden it with a large number of restrictions. The constitution was a broad and flexible document allowing the president to make of the office what he

1. Gompers, "The American Labor Movement," *American Federationist* 21 (July 1914): 537-48. For further material on the organizational structure of the AFL see Lewis L. Lorwin, *The American Federation of Labor* (Washington, D.C.: Brookings Institution, 1933), pp. 301-38; Robert Franklin Hoxie, *Trade Unionsm in the United States* (New York: D. Appleton & Company, 1923), pp. 112-35.
2. Constitution of the American Federation of Labor, Article II.
3. An excellent example of the power of the large national unions is seen in the dispute between the Machinists and the Flint Glass Workers. In eleven conventions, a decision had been rendered in favor of the Flints, but as their delegate stated: "What can we do, with only 10,000 members, when an organization of 180,000 members refuses to abide by the decision?" The convention ordered the Machinists to yield the disputed jurisdiction, but declined to suspend them for refusal to obey. The highest governing body of the Federation virtually pleaded with the Machinists to obey the decisions of the general movement without coercion. In reply, the Machinists, with disdain and a certain lack of concern for a convention mandate, answered that they would "do what they considered right, and nothing else." See *The Seamen's Journal* (July 3, 1918). For a detailed discussion of the national unions and their power within the Federation, see George E. Barnett, "Dominance of the National Union in American Labor Organization," *Quarterly Journal of Economics* 27 (May 1913): 455-81.

would. Personality thus became the key element in the assumption and exercise of power.[4] As a result, personal loyalties developed as the overriding factor in the determination and implementation of policy.

Gompers, from its inception, gave the office a prestige and dignity that enabled him to impress his program on the national unions, particularly in areas such as foreign affairs, which did not impinge on craft autonomy. He dominated the Federation and, as John Frey was to state in 1948: "[He] had an influence on the trade union movement that was exceptional and that has not existed since his time."[5]

Since final authority was vested in the convention, Gompers sought to exercise a large degree of control over this body. He was aided in this by a constitutional provision that gave to the president the right to appoint all members of all committees.[6] The importance of this provision cannot be overlooked since, as the delegates of the Tailors' Industrial Union reported, the real business of the convention was performed in hotel lobbies and committee rooms.[7] Not only did Gompers name the members of a committee; he also determined who was to be its chairman. So arbitrary had his power become that, as Frey admits, he consulted no one in his selection. Once a chairman and committee were selected, Gompers seldom made a change.[8] However, he retained the constitutional authority to remove any committee member who displeased him.

This resulted in committee reports that passively and uncritically accepted the wishes of the leadership. As a member of the Policy Committee, Frey acknowledged that on major questions no report ever came to the floor from this committee with which Gompers was in disagreement.[9] Only on minor questions would an occasional dispute arise. At no time during the war years could I find an instance

4. Lorwin, *American Federation of Labor,* pp. 332, 336-37.
5. Notes of a lecture by John P. Frey, Harvard Student Seminar, May 12, 1948, John P. Frey Manuscripts, Manuscript Division, Library of Congress, Washington, D.C.; *The Survey* (March 25, 1916), p. 759.
6. Constitution of the American Federation of Labor, Article 3, Section 3.
7. *The Tailor* (December 8, 1914). The Tailors' Industrial Union was formerly known as the Journeymen Tailors' Union of America. In 1915, it reverted to its original name.
8. Frey, Harvard Seminar, Frey MSS.
9. *Ibid.*

of a committee concurring in a resolution on foreign affairs that was contrary to the wishes of Samuel Gompers.

The procedure of the convention also made it more difficult for the opposition to pass resolutions opposing the policies of the leadership. All resolutions were referred to committees, and what came before the convention was not the adoption or rejection of the resolution, but the adoption or rejection of the committee's report.[10] Thus the prestige of the committee became an important factor, and many delegates were reluctant to vote against a committee's findings for fear of embarrassing it.

This is not to imply that all recommendations of committees were supported by the convention. Occasionally, the convention would overturn a committee's report. This usually occurred when a committee supported a measure that evoked traditional labor hostility, such as military preparedness. When a resolution to request President Wilson to prevent any further attempt to introduce military training in the schools was reported out of the Committee of International Relations with a recommendation for nonconcurrence, the convention, after a lively debate, voted to reject the committee's report and to adopt the resolution.[11] However, the importance of the act was not so much in what may appear as a rebellion of the convention against Administration policy, as in the fact that the resolution could not have passed without the ardent support of some of Gompers's closest collaborators, especially James Duncan, first vice-president of the AFL. Yet, Duncan's apostasy was to be short-lived. At the next convention, he was vigorously to oppose a similar resolution.[12]

Gompers's heightened interest in foreign affairs became apparent in 1913 when he was instrumental in creating a new committee on international affairs.[13] The importance he attached to this committee soon became evident. In order to insure his preeminence in the field of foreign policy-making he took the unusual step of having himself nominated, each year, as an additional member of this committee. During the war years, no other committee was to be so honored.

10. *The Tailor* (December 11, 1917).
11. AFL, *Proceedings* (1916), pp. 303, 309-10.
12. John A. Fitch, "Organized Labor in War-Time," *The Survey* (December 1, 1917), pp. 232-35.
13. AFL, *Proceedings* (1913), p. 129.

Another factor making for administration support was the composition of the delegates. The national unions were generally run by small groups of office holders who were usually the chosen delegates, year after year, to the AFL conventions. The rank and file had little representation.[14] Together with the officers of the Federation, this group of professional union officials was noted, in 1914, for its increasingly conservative cast.[15] Writing four years later, *The New Republic* was to label these same officials as an "Old Guard . . . not any better adjusted to the revolutionary social and economic needs which the war is developing than is the American Association of Manufacturers."[16] Yet, within such a framework, Gompers operated at his best. His intimate relationships with many of the national officials provided a welcome asset, especially in those areas where personality was an important factor in policy formulation.

In securing the allegiance of the national unions to his foreign-affairs program, Gompers made full use of the parochial outlook of many of the union officers who were concerned solely with "bread and butter" issues without regard for the broader policies affecting workers. They believed that whatever happened outside their own narrow domain, such as international affairs, was peripheral to the real interests of the workingmen and their trade unions.[17] They were content to leave such subjects to the president of the AFL and the Executive Council.

The extent to which Gompers had been able to control the forming and implementing of organized labor's "war program" was frankly admitted by the Machinists. Led by a socialist and rumored to be in controversy with Gompers over his support of the war, the International Association of Machinists, third largest union in the AFL, revealed itself as having been too passive and neglectful in this area.[18] But its solution simply compounded its original error. The Machinists aimed their criticism not at Gompers's general war policies, but at what they regarded as his attempts to define their position in matters

14. *The Tailor* (November 30, 1914).
15. Charles Stelzle, "Labor in Council," *The Outlook* (December 2, 1914), pp. 761-62.
16. *The New Republic* (February 16, 1918), pp. 69-71.
17. *The Tailor* (November 27, 1917).
18. *Machinists' Monthly Journal* 29 (December 1917): 1043-44.

that vitally affected their craft.[19] In effect, they were still willing to leave overall war policy planning to "Sam," but would not tolerate his interference in what they considered to be "bread and butter" questions.

The prevalence of this attitude was highlighted by an editorial in the *Coast Seaman's Journal*, a trade-union paper noted for its nonconformist views on foreign affairs. It takes the San Francisco Labor Council to task for spending so much of its time "with war issues and kindred matters foreign to the real interests of the wageworkers."[20]

Fundamentally, Gompers succeeded in fastening his foreign-policy ideas on the labor movement because, in the words of a pro-war socialist, John Spargo, "he represent[ed] the mass."[21] Gompers was an able advocate of the narrow craft-union policies favored by the officials of the national unions and they, in turn, not having his broad social and political outlook and preferring to concentrate on expanding their own vested interests, were willing to leave all questions on international affairs to the president of the AFL.

The result was that at any convention the Gompers machine was "powerful enough to pass any resolution it want[ed] to pass."[22] As the war eroded socialist strength, the conventions lacked the usual conflict of ideas and became, more and more, pliable bodies conforming to the wishes of the leadership. This remained the pattern during the war years.

The Executive Council was under mandate of the constitution to carry out the decisions of the convention. In doing so, it exercised "wide discretionary and initiatory powers." This has led some to conclude that it was the really powerful executive body of the Federation. However, as it operated during Gompers's tenure, it acted mainly as an advisory body to the president, and was content to give its stamp of approval to programs initiated by him. This was partly due to the fact that Council members had responsibilities in their own

19. *Ibid.*
20. *Coast Seamen's Journal* (May 10, 1916).
21. John Spargo to Benjamin C. Marsh, August 21, 1917, James G. Phelps Stokes Manuscripts, Manuscript Division, Butler Library, Columbia University, New York.
22. *The Tailor* (January 12, 1915).

unions and could not devote themselves wholly to AFL problems. Since the Council met only twice a year, day-to-day affairs were actually in the hands of the president. In substance, the Council found itself more of a body providing constitutional sanction to Gompers's wishes than one that launched programs of its own.

Gompers's assertion of power reached such heights during the war that he frequently employed the technique of acting first and then presenting the Council and union leaders with the accomplished fact, supremely confident that his course of action would be approved. This was usually the case. In deciding to attend a labor conference of Inter-Allied countries, Gompers, acting alone, chose all the AFL delegates, explaining that time prevented his consulting with the Council. He asked the members to approve his selection and officially to designate the group as representative of the American Federation of Labor.[23] They quickly complied.

Of greater import was the manner in which Gompers was able to stamp labor's official endorsement on Wilson's foreign policies, less than a month prior to the president's decision to ask Congress for a declaration of war against Germany. Exercising his authority under Article 6, Section 4, of the AFL Constitution, Gompers issued a call for a special meeting of the Executive Council to take place on March 9, 1917.[24] Within a few days and without prior authorization from the Executive Council, but contingent on its approval, he called for a meeting of the national and international unions and departments affiliated with the Federation on March 12.[25] In his letter to the Council members, Gompers justified his position on the ground that he anticipated that the Executive Council would recognize the existence of an emergency and, in such circumstances, he felt "warranted in assuming that the call [would] receive your approval."[26]

23. Gompers to Executive Council, August 8, 1918, Gompers MSS.
24. Gompers to Executive Council, February 28, 1917, Gompers MSS.
25. Gompers to Executive Council, Presidents of National and International Unions, A. F. of L. Departments and the Unaffiliated Organizations, March 2, 1917, Gompers MSS. It should be noted that in this letter Gompers stated that the meeting called for March 12, 1917, would not take place unless he received authorization from the Executive Council. However, he had set all Federation machinery in motion in anticipation of the meeting and it would have placed an unreasonable burden on the Council at this stage if it refused to sanction the conference.
26. Gompers to Executive Council, February 28, 1917, Gompers MSS.

Again, the Council was faced with a *fait accompli*. And again it meekly acquiesced.

In his Autobiography, Gompers praises his own democratic virtues in the sense that he never presumed to speak for organized labor without proper authorization.[27] However, the facts indicate otherwise. The president of the American Federation of Labor entered into agreements with the government that were clearly beyond his authority.

The first big war contracts were for cantonment construction. The War Department was anxious to come to an agreement with labor so that production could be speeded up and delays averted. In order to accomplish this task, Louis B. Wehle, assistant to Secretary of War Newton D. Baker, sought to reach an agreement with Gompers over wages, hours, and working conditions. The result was the signing of the Baker-Gompers Memorandum.[28] Wehle recognized that "Gompers had to proceed with caution about it, especially because, in signing the memorandum, he was assuming authority that only the national union presidents in the building trades possessed."[29] Furthermore, writes Wehle, "we realized without discussion that it was clearly impracticable for me to enter into protracted negotiations with them over a point so loaded with dynamite."[30] The explosive nature of the agreement lay in the fact that Gompers had, in effect, surrendered the closed shop in return for union wages and hours, an act he was later to categorically substantiate in writing.[31]

The agreement raises an interesting question. What effect or importance did the War Department attach to Gompers's signature, since it recognized his lack of authority to commit labor to such an agreement? Again, Wehle reveals the attitude of the Government: "we felt that the agreement would exert the necessary leverage for subjecting the building-trades unions and their members to its undertakings."[32] Wehle's assessment was correct. Gompers, with the collaboration of

27. Samuel Gompers, *Seventy Years of Life and Labor* (New York: E. P. Dutton and Company, 1925), 2: 359-60.
28. For the text of the memorandum see AFL, *Proceedings* (1917), pp. 82-83.
29. Louis B. Whele, *Hidden Threads of History* (New York: Macmillan Co., 1953), p. 21.
30. *Ibid.*
31. Gompers to Wehle, June 22, 1917, Gompers MSS.
32. Wehle, *Hidden Threads*, p. 23.

the government, acted on the principle that once an act was accomplished it would be difficult for other labor leaders to oppose it because of government pressure and public opinion.[33]

This arbitrary assumption of authority by Gompers, supported and rationalized on the grounds that a national emergency existed, became an established pattern during the war years. In fact, the Wilson Administration was to rely more and more on Samuel Gompers to secure labor's total compliance with its program. Gompers was not in disagreement with such an assessment; he was proud of it. Toward the end of the war, he was to write that "through the organized labor movement American workers have been held in line to cooperate and work thru government agencies. . . ."[34]

Gompers was to employ the same technique in organizing the American Alliance for Labor and Democracy—an organization devoted to combating the pacifist teachings of the "People's Council"—as he had in signing the Baker-Gompers Memorandum. It was the joint product of the Federation chief and the Committee on Public Information, a newly formed government agency responsible for the dissemination and control of propaganda during the war. The Alliance named Gompers as its president and Frank Morrison as its secretary. Its pronouncements were thereupon greeted as the voice of organized labor.

Yet Gompers had no official authority, either to organize the Alliance or to act as its leading officer.[35] No such power was vested in his office to sanction such an undertaking. Gompers was well aware of this and recognized that, at the moment, the Alliance did not officially represent organized labor, but that, in reality, it was difficult for the public to distinguish between the official and unofficial representation.[36] He was plainly pleased that the public regarded the AALD as a spokesman for organized labor.

Reflecting later on his arbitrary use of authority, Gompers more

---

33. In his Autobiography, Gompers states that he simply "assumed responsibility for a course [he] knew was indispensible." See Gompers, *Seventy Years,* 2: 374. This is an obvious contradiction of his earlier statement, where he claimed that he never spoke for organized labor without proper authorization.
34. *American Federationist* 25 (August 1918): 687-90.
35. Gompers, *Seventy Years,* 2: 382.
36. Gompers to Robert Maisel, September 29, 1917, Stokes MSS.

clearly defined his own concept of presidential powers during wartime. Since he had no official authority for his course of action, Gompers defended his role on the basis that he ''had the intrinsic authority arising out of great national need and opportunity to serve.''[37] Using such guidelines, Gompers, in effect, saw the powers of his office during wartime as almost limitless. His ''intrinsic authority'' could be bounded only by internal political considerations, and these were held in check by his astute use of the prestige and powers of his office, by the unstinting support he received from the Wilson Administration, by the inflammable nature of public opinion during wartime, and by an exuberance of patriotic feeling that seemed to overcome many labor leaders.

To gain labor's official endorsement of the Alliance, Gompers sought the approval of the 1917 AFL Convention. Because considerable opposition developed, the leadership had to resort to a familiar tactic. It sought to make the issue one of Gompers's prestige rather than of the Alliance itself. Matthew Woll, an unwavering supporter of Gompers, had to plead with the Convention that failure to approve of the AALD would place the president of the Federation ''in a most unenviable and embarrassing light . . . before our people and the public generally.''[38] As an added argument, a vote against the Alliance was equated with disloyalty to the country and government.[39]

The office of the president of the AFL also had under its jurisdiction two important assets: absolute control over all Federation publications and the complete power to hire and dismiss all AFL general organizers. Gompers utilized each to the fullest extent in promoting his policies.

The *American Federationist,* official journal of the AFL, was edited by Samuel Gompers, who almost single-handedly determined its content. The importance of the magazine lay in the fact that it was the only trade-union publication that had a national circulation and whose views could reach all segments of the labor movement. Opponents of Gompers were frequently excoriated in its pages and

37. Gompers, *Seventy Years,* 2: 382.
38. AFL, *Proceedings* (1917), p. 293.
39. *Ibid.,* p. 295.

were hardly given an opportunity to reply. The editor of the *Machinists' Monthly Journal,* one of the objects of the president's wrath, was finally compelled to devote a major portion of the *Journal* to a rebuttal of the charges made by Gompers.[40] This consumed the time and energy of the staff and diverted its attention from other pressing problems. The effect of such attacks led many editors to conclude that conformity with AFL policies was much safer than dissent.[41]

The power to appoint AFL general organizers enabled Gompers to build up a personal organization of labor officials entirely dependent on him for their jobs.[42] His method of selection was often for the purpose of making alliances within insurgent unions such as the Miners.[43] Gompers could, and did, rely on this group of organizers as an effective instrument in carrying out his program. An example of their importance can be seen in the formation of the AALD. They were instructed by Gompers to devote their entire efforts to see that representative labor men and unions sent delegates to the founding convention of that organization.[44] As events turned out, trade union representation at the conference without their help might have been much more anemic than it was.

Since Gompers was one of the main pillars supporting the Administration's program, Wilson treated him as an unofficial liaison between organized labor and the White House. After America's declaration of war, hardly a month went by without Gompers having several appointments with the president. Requests poured in to Gompers for aid in securing government jobs or commissions in the armed forces, which he dutifully tried to secure for his

---

40. *Machinists' Monthly Journal* 28 (June 1916): 531-35.
41. The AFL also published a *Weekly News Letter,* which supplied information and data on current trade-union activities, and was frequently used by trade-union publications as a source of news and information.
42. Frey voiced the belief that this power of appointment was limited by internal political considerations—the desire of a union wanting to get rid of a man and successfully pressuring Gompers to appoint him to the AFL staff. He cited John L. Lewis as a prime example. See Frey, Harvard Seminar, Frey MSS.
43. Saul Alinsky, *John L. Lewis* (New York: G. P. Putnam & Sons, 1949), pp. 22-23.
44. Gompers to Hugh Frayne, August 29, 1917, War Industries Board Files, 8-A1, National Archives, Washington, D.C.

constituents.[45] It was generally recognized that in order for labor men to see the President, they had to go through Gompers. When the Chicago Federation of Labor, an organization not too enthusiastic over the AFL's war policies, desired to secure a pardon for Frank M. Ryan, president of the Ironworkers who was convicted of conspiracy to ship dynamite in interstate commerce, they were obliged to ask Gompers to make the appointment.[46] Many of the unions, insecure over their own survival and never knowing when they might need a presidential favor, were reluctant to offer any opposition to the Gompers program.[47] In effect, the Government's partisan attitude to Gompers helped strengthen his hold on the administrative machinery of the Federation.

Another source of strength to the AFL leadership was the benevolent attitude shown it, at times, by leading financiers and major industrialists, who agreed with Gompers's support of increased aid for national defense and an Allied victory. During 1915, the president of the Federation had been making charges that strikes in munitions plants were German-inspired. He feared he would be vulnerable to attacks from his opponents on this issue, since he lacked evidence to corroborate his accusations.[48] Gompers sought the aid of Ralph Easley of the National Civic Federation. Easley set up an investigating unit in an effort to seek proof to substantiate Gompers's charges.[49] For funds Easley went to Henry P. Davidson of the J. P. Morgan Co. who raised $25,000 by assessing manufacturers who were making supplies for the Allies $2,500 each.[50] In effect, the leading industrial tycoons of the country were playing an active role in internal

45. Gompers to William B. Wilson, April 2, 1917, Gompers MSS; Gompers to Newton D. Baker, April 5, 1917, Gompers MSS; Gompers to Baker, March 21, 1917, Gompers MSS; Gompers to Baker, May 25, 1917, Gompers MSS; Gompers to Baker, July 17, 1917, Gompers MSS; Gompers to William B. Wilson, August 18, 1917, Gompers MSS; Gompers to Walter Lippman, September 19, 1917, Gompers MSS.
46. E. N. Nockels to Frank Walsh, August 11, 1917, Walsh Manuscripts, Manuscript Division, New York Public Library, New York.
47. Sidney Hillman to Frank Rosenblum, June 2, 1917, cited by Matthew Josephson, *Sidney Hillman: Statesman of American Labor* (Garden City, N. Y.: Doubleday & Co., 1952), p. 161.
48. Draft memorandum by Ralph M. Easley, "German Sabotage Activities in the U. S., 1915-1916," n.d., NCF MSS.
49. *Ibid.*
50. *Ibid.*

union politics by supporting the leadership of the AFL against some of its most active critics. Significantly, it was the issue of foreign policy that brought about such cooperation. To use today's terminology, this may have marked the bare beginnings of the military-industrial-labor complex.

Conformity with the foreign policies of the Wilson Administration became Gompers's primary aim for the labor movement. He sought to bury all labor dissent under an avalanche of patriotism. Commenting on the 1917 Convention, the Journeymen Tailors' representatives noted that although some delegates opposed the conservative policies of the Federation leaders, they were afraid of saying so for "fear of being branded as pro-German and traitors to the country."[51] The Sailors' Union of the Pacific complained that certain labor leaders "no longer concede any trade unionist the right to disagree with them upon any issue relating to the war."[52] To do so was to be considered an act of disloyalty. Many labor officials simply kept quiet, for they were cognizant of the fact that to become identified with policies opposed by Gompers meant an end of any opportunities they may have had for service in the labor movement.[53]

Those who openly defied Gompers found that the entire machinery of the Federation was mobilized in an effort to defeat them. At the annual convention of the Pennsylvania State Federation of Labor, AFL general organizers admitted to James Maurer, a member of the pro-peace People's Council and candidate for reelection as president, that they had been sent by Gompers to work for his defeat.[54] Simultaneously, many officials recommended by Maurer for appointment to positions in the AFL were removed and replaced by other men.[55] The government was made privy to such information and Bernard Baruch, chairman of the War Industries Board, was informed that the situation in New York and Pennsylvania had become so threatening as to warrant a general movement to clear it up.[56] Left unanswered

---

51. *The Tailor* 1 (November 1917): 7.
52. *Coast Seamen's Journal* (September 5, 1917).
53. John Spargo to Benjamin C. Marsh, August 2, 1917, Stokes MSS.
54. James H. Maurer, *It Can Be Done* (New York: The Rand School Press, 1938), p. 229.
55. Memorandum from Hugh Frayne to Bernard Baruch, August 30, 1918, W.I.B. Files, 8-A1, National Archives.
56. *Ibid.*

was the question of the kind of role the government would play in aiding the AFL leadership to purge the dissidents. It is fair to assume that it would be active rather than passive.

Organizations like the United Hebrew Trades, which supported the Amalgamated Clothing Workers of America, a union not recognized by the Federation, and the pro-peace position of the People's Council were threatened by the AFL leadership with virtual extinction. A resolution was introduced at the AFL Convention requiring that all local unions affiliated with the United Hebrew Trades withdraw from membership in that organization.[57] While the leadership avoided taking so drastic a step, its action was not without effect. The secretary of the United Hebrew Trades announced in March of 1918 that henceforth the organization would participate in the third Liberty Loan. This marked a complete reversal of its previous anti-war policy. It was interpreted by many as a move to rob some of its critics of an issue in their attempt to suppress it.[58]

In retrospect, we may conclude that the loose organizational structure of the Federation was an added asset to a strong and aggressive president like Gompers, possessing great prestige and stature among labor men, who desired to identify organized labor's foreign policy totally with that of the Administration in Washington. However, it also becomes clear that without the fervent patriotism generated by a war crisis and the wholehearted support of the government and certain industrial leaders, Gompers might not have been able to move organized labor so successfully in the direction of his stated aims.

57. AFL, *Proceedings* (1917), pp. 381-83.
58. *The Tailor* 2 (March 1918): 2.

3

The Controversy over Neutrality

As the "guns of August" roared and war devastated Europe, America began to ponder its own course of action. When President Wilson issued his official proclamation of neutrality on August 4, 1914, the American people applauded in unison. Few, if any, voices were raised in favor of direct intervention in Europe's conflict.[1] An overwhelming majority of the American public favored a policy of strict neutrality. The debate and controversy that subsequently surfaced in 1915 and 1916 revolved around the question of how best to implement this policy. In a word, was the U.S. to adhere to the traditional rules of international law and demand the right of freedom of trade with all the belligerents, or, conversely, was the Administration, cognizant of British control of the seas and the importance of Allied trade to the American economy, to accept the British maritime system, which violated traditional neutral rights and worked to the disadvantage of the Central Powers. The president of the U.S. and

1. Even so ardent a champion of the Allied cause as former President Theodore Roosevelt regarded it as "folly to jump into the gulf ourselves. . . ." For a discussion of initial reaction to the war see Arthur S. Link, *Wilson: The Struggle for Neutrality, 1914-1915* (Princeton: Princeton University Press, 1960), 3: 1-56; Charles Seymour, *American Diplomacy During the World War* (Baltimore: The Johns Hopkins Press, 1934), pp. 1-8.

the president of the AFL again found themselves in accustomed agreement; both chose the latter course.

Declaring that it would be bound by "the existing rules of international law," the United States reserved to itself the right to ship noncontraband goods to any of the belligerents or to a neutral port. But the British clamped a tight blockade around Germany and neutral Europe, and carried out a policy of harassing American merchantmen and of generally ignoring conventional rules of international law.[2] Clearly, such acts were destined to increase friction between the two nations. At the same time, the Allies had come to the conclusion that the blockade, as well as American goods and finance, was essential to victory. Thus, the main objective of its diplomacy was ". . . to secure the maximum of blockade that could be enforced without a rupture with the United States."[3]

That the Administration in Washington did not desire such a "rupture" soon become apparent. Wilson was reluctant to press the British on their disregard of neutral rights but displayed no such latitude when it came to German violations.[4] Coupled with the fact that the United States was becoming a huge military arsenal for Allied war material as well as a center of financial support, United States policy did not affect the belligerents equally. It was inevitably moving this country closer and closer to war with the Central Powers.[5] As a result, it was to unloose a storm of controversy within the country over what many regarded as a policy destined to involve the United States in the war. In the ensuing debate over neutrality, the position of organized labor assumed particular importance.

Gompers's advocacy of the government's position on neutrality was not derived from a concern for legal niceties, nor was it grounded on a sincere desire to keep the United States aloof from the European struggle. Almost from its inception, he regarded the war as

---

2. For a discussion of neutral rights and the British Maratime system see Arthur S. Link, *American Epoch* (New York: Alfred A Knopf, 1966), pp. 171-81.
3. Edward Grey (Viscount Grey of Falloden), *Twenty-Five Years, 1892-1916* (New York: Frederick A. Stokes, 1925), 2:107.
4. Joseph P. Tumulty, *Woodrow Wilson As I Knew Him* (New York: Garden City Publishing, 1925), p. 229.
5. For an analysis of the impact of United States policy, see Ray Stannard Baker, *Woodrow Wilson: Life and Letters* (Garden City, N.Y.: Doubleday, Doran and Company, 1937), 6:121; Seymour, *American Diplomacy*, p. 12; Frederick L. Paxson, *Pre-War Years, 1913-1917* (Boston: Houghton, Mifflin Company, 1936), pp. 202-3.

THE CONTROVERSY OVER NEUTRALITY/49

a conflict between democratic ideals and autocratic militarism. Gompers saw the Allies not only as protectors of American institutions, but also as defenders of a labor movement fashioned along AFL lines. To aid their cause, he quietly worked to subvert any program that sought to implement a policy of neutrality in deed as well as in word. Our policy of neutrality was, to Gompers, merely a subterfuge to support the Allies.[6] As his confidential assistant was later to write: "He was quite oblivious to Great Britain's invasion of our freedom on the high seas but . . . [he] recounted vividly damages to our shipping and losses of American lives by German submarines. He seemed personally committed to aid Great Britain. . . ."[7]

President Wilson, like Gompers, did not view the war in Europe with impartial detachment. He regarded England as "fighting our fight," and was apprehensive over the prospect of a German victory, which he felt "would change the course of civilization and make the United States a military power." Thus, both passionately favored the Allies. Yet slight differences in emphasis between the two did emerge. Labor, as it was to do with disturbing frequency in the future, developed a policy that was less neutral and more pro-interventionist than the Administration was ready to advocate at the time. While Wilson, recognizing the force of peace sentiment among the American people in 1915, did not feel justified in "bringing them into a war which they do not understand,"[8] Gompers had already reached the conclusion that "it was not possible for any important world-power to remain neutral."[9] As the war dragged on, the

6. Gompers never tired of seeking to justify our policy of neutrality. After our entrance into the war, in speech after speech he defended this policy as being truly neutral and impartial. See Samuel Gompers, *American Labor and the War* (New York: George H. Doran Co., 1919), pp. 91-92.
7. Florence Calvert Thorne, *Samuel Gompers—American Statesman* (New York: Philosophical Library, 1957), p. 146.
8. Charles Seymour, *The Intimate Papers of Colonel House* (Boston and New York: Houghton Mifflin Company, 1928), 1:293; Tumulty, *Wilson*, p. 231. Also, Seymour, *Intimate Papers*, 2:50; Link, *Wilson*, 3:51.
9. Samuel Gompers, *Seventy Years of Life and Labor* (New York: E. P. Dutton and Co., 1919), 2:334. In a number of speeches after the United States entered the conflict, Gompers described his impatience at the hesitancy and unwillingness of President Wilson to enter the war earlier but, as a good citizen, he was willing to yield to the judgment of the commander-in-chief. See speech under the auspices of the National Security League, September 14, 1917, and at a reception tendered to the American Federation of Labor Mission by the American Luncheon Club, September 26, 1918, in Gompers, *American Labor and the War*, pp. 121, 239.

president of the AFL was to adopt a tone of belligerency equal to that of the most ardent war proponents and, at times, far surpassing that of the Wilson Administration.

The ever-increasing severity and effectiveness of the British blockade was gradually forcing Germany to seek an adequate response to Britain's control of the seas. Inevitably, the German high command came to regard the submarine as an appropriate weapon for attacking British Commerce. On February 4, 1915, the German Admiralty declared that all enemy merchant ships in the waters around Great Britain would be sunk, and that neutral ships could not be guaranteed a safe passage.[10]

While Wilson's strong objections to the German note—offering "to hold the Imperial German Government to a strict accountability for such acts"—caused Germany to subsequently modify its position, German naval action was making it virtually impossible for the United States to take any position that did not adversely affect one of the belligerents.

An incident was to occur shortly that jolted American opinion and brought closer to home the horrors of war. On May 7, the passenger liner *Lusitania* was sunk by a German submarine with a loss of 124 American lives.[11] The ensuing crisis did serve to clarify existing opinions within the Wilson Administration. It strengthened the conviction of Colonel Edward M. House, intimate adviser to the president, and Robert Lansing, the future secretary of state, that a German victory was inimical to the best interests of the United States. Colonel House had also arrived at the conclusion that "we can no longer remain neutral spectators."[12]

In sharp disagreement with House and Lansing and also with President Wilson, William Jennings Bryan, the secretary of state, charged that the Administration's policy of neutrality was not impartial in its application but was decidedly biased in favor of the Allies. Fearful that Wilson would continue to embrace his present policies on neutrality, and, more specifically, that his second note to Germany over

10. The challenge of the submarine and its effect on relations between Germany and the United States is adequately discussed by Link, *Wilson*, 3:309-67.
11. A full discussion of the *Lusitania* crisis can be found in Link, *Wilson*, 3: 368-455.
12. Cited in *ibid.*, p. 375.

the sinking of the *Lusitania* might embroil the nation in war, Bryan resigned from the Cabinet and went forth to rally the people in behalf of peace.

The division of opinion within the Administration was also reflected within the AFL. Gompers was critical of his old political friend and ally, Bryan, and stood squarely behind President Wilson. At the other end of the spectrum, large sections of organized labor responded warmly to Bryan, and began to regard Wilson's foreign policies as dangerously provocative. Opposition to the Administration's position was not confined to the rank and file but also embraced many in leadership positions.

Bryan's resignation was reflective of the depth of peace sentiment in the nation. In fact, as Professor Link indicates, so widespread was the demand for peace that Wilson became convinced he would have to find some peaceful settlement of the *Lusitania* affair.[13] It was a classic case of public opinion's affecting foreign policy decisions. The question remains as to the extent of organized labor's involvement in the peace crusade and its influence on public opinion as well as on the mind of Woodrow Wilson.

Sensing the imminent possibility of American involvement over the *Lusitania* crisis, a clamor arose in the country for a reinterpretation of the rules of neutrality. Specifically, the demand for an embargo of all goods to any of the belligerents began to gain in popularity. However, an embargo would have been almost fatal to any chance the Allies entertained of a final victory as well as seriously damaging an American economy that was just beginning to surge forward on the strength of Allied war orders. As such, it was to incur the bitter hostility of Woodrow Wilson and Samuel Gompers. However, organized labor, despite the importance of a strengthened economy to its membership, did not march in unison behind the president of the AFL.

Prior to the sinking of the *Lusitania,* elements within the AFL had already begun to make their position clear on neutrality. In April, a meeting held under the auspices of the Central Federated Union in New York and chaired by Morris Braun, secretary of the Cigarmak-

---

13. *Ibid.*, p. 441.

ers' Union, issued a call for an embargo and endorsed a resolution "for a general strike among those industries employed in the production of ammunition and food supplies destined for any of the belligerents."[14]

However, the uproar over the sinking of the *Lusitania* served to accelerate trade-union activity in behalf of peace. The Sailors' Union of the Pacific sought to partially justify Germany's action and undermine any demand for war over the issue by publicly charging that the *Lusitania* was not only a passenger vessel but "had in her hold military goods valued at more than a quarter of a million dollars."[15] At the same time, the union placed its complete faith in Woodrow Wilson and expressed a willingness to accept his advice.

On May 27, nine international unions with headquarters in Indianapolis—United Mine Workers, International Typographical Union, Stone Cutters, Bricklayers, Carpenters, Book Binders, Structural Iron Workers, and Barbers—met at the headquarters of the United Mine Workers to voice their opposition to war in general and urged the government to do everything possible to keep the country out of the European conflict.[16] The meeting was of the utmost importance. All the attending trade unions were affiliated with the AFL and represented approximately 900,000 members. Its views were broad based and thus reflective of wide sections of the leadership and membership of the labor movement. Furthermore, Gompers could not dismiss lightly the opinions of some of the most powerful trade-union leaders. He was reluctant to attack the conference openly. At its conclusion, the conference asked Gompers to call a meeting of all labor organizations if the United States should reach the point of becoming involved in the war.[17] Gompers, despite many promises, never

14. *New York Times,* April 16, 1915, p. 4. The presence of Braun is significant because it illustrates that, even in unions like the Cigarmakers, which followed the leadership of the AFL in foreign affairs and whose president, G. W. Perkins, was chosen by Gompers at every convention to be chairman of the International Relations Committee, sizable elements of the staff and rank and file remained in opposition.

15. *Coast Seamen's Journal* (May 19, 1915). The Union, a staunch anti-war advocate, editorialized against accepting a strict pacifist position. It was against war but would "not refuse to sanction war if that be necessary to maintain humanity."

16. Lewis L. Lorwin, *The American Federation of Labor* (Washington, D.C.: Brookings Institution, 1933), p. 140; *The Outlook* (June 30, 1915), pp. 482-83.

17. *Ibid.*

obliged.[18] He received similar requests from the Maintenance of Way Employees' Union, the Commercial Telegraphers' Union, the Chicago Federation of Labor, and the Pennsylvania State Federation of Labor, but continued to ignore them all.[19]

The Women's Trade Union League, after listening to an address by Gompers, resolved to "resist with all their power any attempt to embroil the United States in the conflict now devastating Europe." The League went on to urge the president and Congress "to place an embargo upon the exportation of arms . . . to any other country."[20]

At a Carnegie Hall meeting in June, sponsored by organized labor, Bryan's call for peace was seconded by Joseph Cannon of the Western Federation of Miners, Ernest Bohm of the Central Federated Union, and Joseph P. Holland of the International Brotherhood of Firemen. Samuel Gompers refused to attend, implying that the meeting would place the labor movement in a false position. He did not see any need for a peace meeting since he believed that the United States government was doing everything possible to keep out of the conflict. If the United States should enter the war, Gompers was adamant in his insistence that labor would unite behind the Administration. Essentially, Gompers's position was to have full faith and trust in Woodrow Wilson, a position with which the president of the United States was naturally in full accord.

Gompers gave copies of his reply to the press and it received wide publicity. He intended it as labor's definitive statement on war policy. Wilson expressed his appreciation for Gompers's stand and encouraged his opposition to labor's involvement with any peace organization.[21]

The importance of Gompers's statement could not have been lost on Wilson. It created a barrier between the peace movement and organized labor and prevented the former from utilizing the organizational structure of the Federation to solidify its position among the workingmen. Furthermore, it committed the AFL leadership not only to support Wilson's present course of action against Germany, but

18. Gompers to William Green, June 4, 1915, Gompers MSS.
19. Lorwin, *American Federation of Labor,* p. 140.
20. *New York Times,* June 13, 1915, p. 6.
21. Gompers to Ernest Bohm, June 18, 1915, enclosed in a letter from Gompers to Woodrow Wilson, June 28, 1915, Wilson MSS;*New York Times,* June 20, 1915, p. 1.

pledged itself in advance to support whatever position the president was to take as a consequence of this action. The net effect was to give Wilson a freer hand in interpreting America's policy on neutrality.

An attempt further to stimulate the peace movement among organized labor was undertaken on June 22 with the organization of Labor's National Peace Council. It was led by Representative Frank Buchanan of Illinois and numbered among its officers important labor officials—Milton Snellings of Steam and Operating Engineers; William F. Krower, general secretary-treasurer of Brotherhood of Blacksmiths and Helpers; Rudolph Modest of Amalgamated Meat Cutters; Jacob C. Taylor, secretary-treasurer of Federated Central Body of the States of New York and New Jersey; L. P. Straube, business manager of Commercial Portrait Artists; Ernest Bohm, secretary of Central Federated Union of New York; and Fred Lohn of the Leather Workers' Union.[22] The Council opposed any move to involve America in the war, favored strict neutrality and government ownership of war patents, and sought to prevent financial loans to the Allies. During the early stages of its organization, despite many difficulties and much hostility, the Council attracted a sufficient number of men whose names and positions gave considerable weight to their opinions.[23] It was a force that could not be ignored.

The creation of Labor's National Peace Council dealt the final blow to Gompers's contention that the AFL was united behind his policies. Dissension was apparent even among Gompers's inner circle. A well-known labor leader, who was described as wielding influence in the Federation second only to that of Gompers, was quoted as being in sharp disagreement with his chief and stating that "Americans should not travel on ships carrying contraband." He supported former Secretary of State Bryan's efforts to achieve peace with honor.[24] The position of labor in the current crisis was becom-

---

22. *Textile Worker* (May 1916), pp. 22-29. Additional labor supporters were Joseph Cannon of the Western Federation of Miners, John Golden of the Textile Workers, and Homer D. Call of the Amalgamated Meat and Butcher Workmen's Union. See Lorwin, *American Federation of Labor*, p. 139.

23. *New York Times,* May 7, 1917, p. 8.

24. *The Outlook* (July 7, 1915), pp. 549-50. The reluctance of union officials who disagreed with Gompers foreign policies to identify themselves publicly developed into a pattern of behavior during the war years. This may have been due either to a sense of personal loyalty to the chief or to a fear of antagonizing such a powerful figure as Gompers.

ing a matter of concern to the country. To many, organized labor appeared to be veering toward pacifism. The fact that many labor unions passed resolutions against war and labor men constituted a large element in the anti-war meetings of former Secretary of State William Jennings Bryan, supported this attitude.[25] After analyzing the situation, *The Outlook* came to the conclusion that American labor as a whole was not any more pacifist or militant than the rest of the country.[26] However, in the summer of 1915, aside from the response of the German and Irish cultural societies, the appeal for an arms embargo was truly national in character. From the response of the labor unions, and the presence of labor men in the various peace groups, it would be fair to assume that, despite the opposition of the AFL hierarchy, substantial sections of organized labor played a vanguard role in creating this sentiment.

Substantiating labor's important role in the peace movement, the Friends of Peace, a federation of organizations opposed to America's entry into the war, issued a call for a National Peace Convention to be held in Chicago on Labor Day, 1915. The object of the Convention was "to urge the early convening of Congress for the purpose of considering an embargo on the exportation of war supplies. . . ."[27] The list of union officials, all affiliated with the AFL, signing the call was impressive: Homer D. Call, president, New York State Federation of Labor; John Golden, president, United Textile Workers; Charles Dodd, president, Piano, Organ and Musical Instrument Workers' Union; Timothy Healy, president, Brotherhood of Stationary Firemen; Ernest Slattery, general organizer, Horseshoers' International Union; and John Sullivan, vice-president, United Brewery Workers. The Upholsterers' International Union of America later added its name.[28]

The British were well aware that the forces in favor of peace were assuming considerable dimensions, and posed a direct threat to the exportation of arms. They were also concerned about the possibility of large-scale strikes in the munitions plants. Either of the above

25. *Ibid.*
26. *Ibid.*
27. *The Tailor* (August 10, 1915).
28. *Ibid.* The position of Timothy Healy is uncertain and confusing. He is listed in the above as a supporter of the Friends of Peace while he is quoted in *The Outlook* (June 30, 1915), p. 483, as a bitter antagonist of the peace movement.

types of action the British considered as likely to be extremely damaging to their cause. The British ambassador wrote to the Foreign Office placing his full faith in Samuel Gompers and urged that "means . . . be taken to bring home to him how fatal the action of the Labor Unions may be."[29] Gompers was not to disappoint the Allies. Faced with increasing peace sentiment in the unions, he used the full powers at his command to retrieve many of the labor men caught in the pacifist net. In this endeavor, he was to be largely successful.

Gompers's attack on proponents of an embargo was varied in its extremes. As an ardent practitioner of the pragmatic philosophy, his means were not always fashioned along ethical lines but were, in the main, determined by the degree of success that they could achieve. As a result, he found one of his most successful weapons in exploiting the twin issues of patriotism and subversion.

Gompers was not reluctant to imply ulterior motives to those who disagreed with him. When asked by a journalist about representatives of labor holding peace meetings in New York, he replied "that it would be extremely interesting to find out who is paying the rent for the halls in which they gather."[30] In his Autobiography, Gompers writes of every peace group during this period as either being financed or duped by the Germans. His story of his struggle against pacificism reads like some fictional spy thriller. He constantly refers to his private and confidential sources of information and his struggle to unearth German agents at work in the labor movement.[31]

Responding to the charge of critics that United States policies were, in effect, a breach of neutrality, Gompers sought to justify the position of President Wilson and the AFL on moral and legal grounds. He refused to equate neutrality with an embargo or to interpret it to mean that the American workingman should refuse to work on war goods. Labor, he declared, was "concerned only with the processes of production for which [it was] paid," and wholly indifferent as to the destination of these goods.[32] He regarded the position

29. Cecil Spring-Rice to Edward Grey, June 10, 1915, Stephen Gwynn, ed., *The Letters and Friendships of Sir Cecil Spring-Rice* (Boston and New York: Houghton Mifflin Company, 1929), 2:272-73.
30. *The Outlook* (July 7, 1915), p. 550.
31. For Gompers's account of his work during this period, see Gompers, *Seventy Years*, 2:334-49.
32. Gompers, *Seventy Years*, 2:337.

of the United States Government as similar to that of the working-man. The United States, Gompers proclaimed, was also indifferent as to the destination of these goods and was willing to sell to any belligerent who desired to become a purchaser. Gompers viewed an embargo as depriving Great Britain of the natural advantage she enjoyed as mistress of the seas. Such a step, in his mind, would be a violation of neutrality as defined by international law.[33]

By the summer of 1915, Gompers had reached the point where he regarded aid to the Allies as one of labor's first priorities. He saw the production of munitions as a "perfectly legitimate" and desirable enterprise, and undertook to use his vast influence to prevent strikes in war industries.[34] His attitude was of significance to the business community and to the Allies. Ralph Easley of the National Civic Federation thought it so important that he notified the British Embassy and wrote to its ambassador that he was "arranging, quietly and informally, for Mr. Gompers to meet four or five leading manufacturers of munitions of war at luncheon."[35] Guy Tripp, chairman of the board of directors of Westinghouse, thought that this was of great significance.[36] Other munitions manufacturers also indicated to Easley their desire to work closely with Gompers.[37] The NCF thus appears to be the catalyst that brought about a working relationship between the president of the AFL, the leading industrialists of the country, and the British Embassy. Again, it is interesting to note that the birth of such unity was derived from the AFL's preeminent interest in foreign affairs, while the employer's predominant concern was with the economics of the situation. Such understandings usually resulted in sacrifices by the union rank and file with, as events were later to prove, few lasting benefits to organized labor.

Strikes in munitions plants, whatever the reason, became anathema to Gompers. He was true to his word to do all in his power to prevent their occurrence. In July 1915, the workers at the Remington Arms Company plant in Bridgeport walked off the job. The trouble originally started as a jurisdictional dispute between millwrights and carpenters, but the Machinists' Union, taking advantage of the situa-

33. *Ibid.*
34. Ralph M. Easley to Sir Cecil Spring-Rice, July 8, 1915, NCF MSS.
35. *Ibid.*
36. *Ibid.*
37. Easley to Gompers, July 8, 1915, NCF MSS.

tion, declared they would strike all Bridgeport plants in support of the eight-hour day.

The Remington Arms plant in Bridgeport was in charge of Major Walter F. Penfield, United States Army, retired, and several other army and navy officers associated with him. Penfield immediately charged that "German influences were back of the strike."[38] As if to support the Company, the newspapers published a statement by Gompers that "offers of money had been made to labor men in Bridgeport to force the strike."[39] The next day Gompers was again reiterating, without mentioning Bridgeport, that strikes were the result of foreign propaganda "seeking to check the manufacture and exportation of supplies for Europe."[40]

When challenged by the president of the Machinists' Union for an explanation of his statement "that German money is being used in American labor troubles," Gompers was forced to retreat. He never retracted his charge of the corrupting influence of German agents in strikes, but simply absolved some of the officers of the international unions engaged in the Bridgeport strike.[41] Commenting on his allegations, *The Outlook* concluded that "not a scintilla of evidence" had been brought forth to prove his contention and that the trouble in Bridgeport was "purely a class affair."[42] The effect of Gompers's charges, according to J. J. Kepler, vice-president of the Machinists' Union, was to weaken the effort of the unions to expand their drive for an eight-hour day.[43]

Gompers also employed the technique of identifying the peace groups with the internal political opponents of many of the union officials and of the labor movement in general. In his analysis of the peace meeting held in New York City under the auspices of the Central Federated Union, the Federation chief reported to the Executive Council that he was convinced that "it was simply another movement of the Socialist political partisans who tried to embarrass and injure our movement."[44] This had the effect of placing the advocates

38. *New York Times,* July 16, 1915, pp. 1-2.
39. *Ibid.*
40. *Ibid.*
41. Gompers to Ernest Bohm, July 28, 1915, Gompers MSS; AFL, *Weekly News Letter,* August 7, 1915; *New York Times,* July 24, 1915, p. 5.
42. *The Outlook* (July 28, 1915), pp. 690-91.
43. *New York Times,* January 12, 1916, p. 22.
44. *American Federationist* 22 (June 1915), p. 451.

of strict neutrality in the uncomfortable position of being willing opponents of the trade-union principles and organization as interpreted by the majority of labor officialdom. It was not calculated to win many friends for the peace movement among labor leaders.

As Allied orders for goods increased, the unemployment of 1914 gradually gave way to a period of relative prosperity in 1915. Unions began to anticipate a large growth in membership.[45] Labor thus became an indirect beneficiary of the war. Nevertheless, many labor men had taken a position in favor of an embargo on the grounds that whoever supplied the implements of war was partly to blame for the war itself. The question of an embargo, therefore, had the ingredients of a struggle between idealism and pragmatism. Gompers sought to exploit the latter. At the 1915 Convention, the Executive Council opposed an embargo, arguing that its implementation would have a disastrous effect on workers by resulting in the closing of many industries which, in turn, would lead to large-scale unemployment and starvation for thousands of working men and their families.[46] The implication of the Council's decision was to create a correlation between war and economic prosperity. The echoes of this position can be heard to the present day.

Gompers's role during the first two years of the war was to provide labor support for existing United States policy on neutrality. However, such a policy, by itself, only promised a continuation of the war without any foreseeable benefits to the working people at its conclusion. As labor unrest over this policy grew, Gompers sought to justify his position by infusing the country's foreign policy with a purpose and objective that would be in accord with the heartfelt wishes of the American people. The Executive Council in its report to the 1915 Convention stressed the following as representing AFL policy:

> The war was caused by conditions and influences for which we are not responsible and the beginning of which it is not our mission to discuss. . . .Only by holding aloof from all movements . . . can the labor movement be in a position to be most helpful in the constructive work of preparing regulations for international adjustments. The matters with which we are mainly con-

45. *Machinists' Monthly Journal* 27 (December 1915), p. 1073.
46. AFL, *Proceedings* (1915), p. 49.

cerned and which it is our duty to help determine, are those things which have to do with reorganization at the close of the war and the establishment of agencies to maintain international justice and therefore permanent peace between nations.[47]

The Council continued its support of the 1914 Convention's call for a Labor Peace Congress to meet at the same time and place that a general congress would be held at the close of the European war to discuss terms of peace. It was of the opinion that a Labor Congress would have great weight in influencing the decisions of the World Congress.

In effect, the AFL ruled out any role for labor in helping to put an end to the European conflict or for using its influence to affect the direction of Wilson's policies. Instead, it committed itself to a program whose objectives could be reached only at the termination of the war and at a time when organized labor's ability to influence events would be minimal. Furthermore, by advocating such nebulous concepts as ". . . justice and right rather than peace at any price," it predicated the entire AFL program upon a successful conclusion of the war. Since international justice and morality could be obtained only through a victor's peace, the Federation's position inevitably led to its abandonment of any policy supporting neutrality in favor of our gradual involvement in the war. It placed the hopes of mankind on the World Peace Congress to be convened after the war. As a result, Gompers viewed all peace movements as detrimental to the welfare of humanity and favored acceptance of Wilson's leadership as the only means to achieve a democratic peace. But the rank and file of labor in 1915 was not ready to accept meekly a non-participatory role on the question of war and peace. As the "preparedness" program of the Wilson Administration began to take shape, labor was to become even more articulate in its opposition.

Perhaps Daniel Tobin, president of the Teamsters, best summed up the mood of labor when he wrote: ". . . we want it distinctly understood that the working people of this country . . . do not desire any war with the European countries unless we are forced into it in defense of our own shores."[48]

47. *Ibid.*, p. 51.
48. *Official Magazine–International Brotherhood of Teamsters, Chauffeurs, Stablemen and Helpers of America* 12 (September 1915): 9; hereafter referred to as *Official Magazine—Teamsters*.

4

Labor and the Struggle over Rearmament

No sooner had the cataclysm of war descended on Europe in 1914 than forces in the United States began to agitate for substantial increases in America's armed forces. Foremost in this movement were prominent members of the military, the large metropolitan press and sections of the industrial establishment located principally in the northeast, and leading figures in the Congress. In the vanguard of the propaganda for more "preparedness" stood the irrepressible leader of the Rough Riders, the hero of the charge up San Juan Hill and ex-president of the United States, Theodore Roosevelt.

Pressure was exerted early on Woodrow Wilson to vastly expand the military capacity of the country. This course of action was urged upon him by one of his closest advisors. When Colonel House suggested in November 1914 that the president form a reserve army, Wilson emphatically registered his dissent, giving as his principal reason the opposition of labor groups who, he acknowledged, felt that a large army was inimical to their interests.[1] Labor was playing an increasingly important role in its support of Wilsonian policies and the president, as a political leader, had simply voiced his reluctance to offend an interest group that proved to be such a strong pil-

---

1. Charles Seymour, *The Intimate Papers of Colonel House* (Boston and New York: Houghton Mifflin Co., 1928), 1: 298.

lar of support in his struggles with the opposition party. Besides, Wilson had little taste for military glamor and saw no necessity for military preparedness at the time.

By the summer of 1915, Wilson gradually, imperceptibly, and in almost circumspect manner, began to veer away from the program so ardently championed by the pacifists and moved closer to a policy that placed greater emphasis on what he was proud to term "reasonable preparedness." It was not the man who had changed, but the external political environment, which had become so altered as to affect the president's thinking. The question of national defense was becoming the foremost issue in the country. With both major parties girding for the coming national elections, Tumulty was to write to his boss that "our all is staked upon a successful issue in this matter."[2] Meanwhile, Colonel House had also arrived at the conclusion that the president "was lost unless he got on the bandwagon of preparedness."[3]

It was not until November that Wilson advocated before the American people a program of military preparedness. The plan called for an expansion of the Regular Army, a slight increase in federal assistance to the National Guard, and the creation of a new reserve Continental Army of 400,000 men. In his opening speech, the president sought to link preparedness with peace. "We have it in our mind to be prepared," he stated, "not for war, but only for defense . . . that the principles we hold most dear be achieved . . . only in the kindly and wholesome atmosphere of peace, and not by the use of hostile force."[4]

However, the forces in movement against war were not to be soothed by the honeyed words of the president in behalf of peace. Perhaps their feelings could best be summed up in the words of Eugene V. Debs, who caustically commented that "any nation which PREPARES for war INCITES war and slaughter."[5] As a result, a thunderous roar of disapproval greeted the president's address. Scores

2. Arthur S. Link, *Wilson, Confusions and Crisis, 1915-1916* (Princeton: Princeton University Press, 1964), 4:45.
3. Cited by Walter Millis, *Road to War* (Boston and New York: Houghton Mifflin Co., 1935), p. 209.
4. Cited by Link, *Wilson*, 4:21.
5. Cited by Ray Ginger, *The Bending Cross* (New Brunswick, N. J.: Rutgers University Press, 1949), p. 329.

of mass meetings were held throughout the land denouncing Wilson's plan as a monstrous plot to militarize America. Clergymen, populists, progressives, farmer groups, and labor unions joined in a common cause to defeat the Administration's program. In the forefront of the opposition was the erstwhile apostle of peace, the Great Commoner, William Jennings Bryan, who was to wage a knightly crusade against the demons of war. Backed by a solid bloc of fifty congressmen, it was poignant reminder that any preparedness legislation presented to Congress by the president was in trouble.

Wilson, aware of the obstacles in his path and concerned lest he provide the Republicans with a campaign issue in an election year, decided to go before the country to explain his plan for national defense. He was convinced that once the issue was clarified before the American people they would join him in urging congressional approval. Of vital concern to the White House was the attitude of the rural farmer and urban worker. Both manifested an implacable hostility to any plan that entailed an increase in the nation's armed forces. In appealing to the workingmen and their unions, Wilson possessed one great advantage: he had the unqualified support of the president of the AFL, Samuel Gompers.

Organized labor's opposition to the military was deeply ingrained, emotional, a part of its folklore, and based on historical experiences. Anti-militarism was as much a part of the ideology of the working man as craft unionism was an integral part of the American Federation of Labor. Labor not only mistrusted the military and its ethic, but feared it as a "clear and present" danger to its own general welfare.

Prior to World War I, all sections of the labor movement fought with a rare display of harmony against any measure that sought to increase the size of America's armed forces. Not until the European war were any sharp divisions in the Federation's rank to spring forth over this issue. As Wilson's drive for "reasonable preparedness" gained momentum in 1915 and 1916, the unity of organized labor was dissolved under the relentless political pressure of the government, the support of the Gompers forces for the Administration's program of rearmament, and the ensuing economic prosperity, which took the sting out of the opposition of some union leaders who were in a state of euphoria over the sudden growth of union membership. Yet, despite the urging of Wilson and Gompers, the overwhelming majority of the rank and file, as well as the officers of the national unions, did not lend their endorsement to the preparedness drive.

Labor's disenchantment with preparedness was based on its conviction that modern wars were mainly imperialistic and brought about by bankers, industrialists, and munitions makers for economic gain. Above all, labor was concerned over whether the war was being used as an excuse to create a large standing army with the express purpose of using it as an instrument to stifle union organization. As far back as 1892, Gompers had charged that the militia was being employed as a "machine of monopolistic oppression against labor," and that the AFL would eventually be forced to "declare that membership in a labor organization and the militia at one and the same time [was] inconsistent and incompatible."[6] Gompers was caustic in his criticism of the War Department which, he claimed, sought to make militarism attractive by establishing military camps for college students during the vacation period. Speaking before the National Civic Federation in 1911, Gompers demanded that the "armed naval and military forces be limited and restricted rather than expanded and extended." The AFL president was in favor of reordering national priorities. "Instead of the enormous expenditures for arsenals and armories, battleships and navy yards," Gompers declared, "we would have them devoted to schoolrooms, colleges, and universities; to university extensions, manual training, and technology; to make parks and playgrounds, air spaces, breathing spaces; to weed out misery and poverty," and to end disease which afflicts the masses of the people.[7]

In the month preceding the outbreak of war, Gompers editorialized that one of the most dangerous tendencies of American industrial society was the use of military men to hamper the labor movement. He regarded these forces as acting solely in the interest of the big business corporations.[8] It was the fear of a large standing army that

6. Annual Report to AFL Convention, December 1892, in Samuel Gompers, *Labor and Common Welfare* (New York: E. P. Dutton and Company, 1919), pp. 239-40; *American Federationist* 21 (February 1919): 122-25.
7. Address at National Civic Federation Conference, January 12, 1911, in Gompers, *Common Welfare*, pp. 220-21.
8. *American Federationist* 21 (August 1914): 636.

proved to be the major roadblock in moving organized labor toward a pro-preparedness position.

Yet, at the same time that Gompers was voicing labor's fear of the military, he had already begun to waver in his opposition to a stronger army and navy. John P. Frey, editor of the *Moulder's Journal* and a close associate of Gompers, stated that as far back as 1911 or 1912 Gompers, in private conversations, was abandoning pacifism "because he saw in the armed camp Europe was becoming a menace to the free institutions of Western Europe."[9] With Gompers's foreknowledge and support, Frey recalled, a resolution was introduced at the 1911 or 1912 AFL convention which, while expressing the basic objections to a large army, supported its development as a necessity to protect our freedoms and liberties.[10] Gompers's failure to campaign openly and forcefully for his position was due to his recognition that the course he desired to pursue would evoke enormous opposition within organized labor and, particularly during the preparedness controversy, if he were to lead the AFL into closer support of President Wilson's policies, political discretion demanded that his public utterances not necessarily reflect his private inclinations.

Labor's doubts as to the real reasons behind preparedness were not entirely groundless. As if to confirm its suspicions, ex-President Taft, a firm proponent of rearmament, in a speech on December 19, 1914, affirmed that a large standing army was necessary for internal order so as to be able to control "riots, mobs and insurrections which cannot be regulated except by the presence of an army."[11] To the United Mine Workers, "Mr. Taft [had] innocently betray[ed] the real cause for which armies [were] everywhere maintained."[12] The Miners favored a foreign policy that would make increased armaments unnecessary and useless. It was to be based on "our isolated geographic position" which, the union believed, would keep us out of any war if we would "just refrain from 'butting in.' "[13]

Isolationist sentiment went hand in hand with the desire of the

9. Notes of a lecture by John P. Frey at Harvard Student Seminar, May 12, 1948, John P. Frey Manuscripts, Manuscript Division, Library of Congress, Washington, D.C.
10. *Ibid.*
11. Cited by *United Mine Workers' Journal* (December 3, 1914), pp. 4-5.
12. *Ibid.*
13. *Ibid.*

overwhelming majority of unions to prevent, at all costs, the establishment of a large standing army. Preparedness was viewed as a scheme to change our historic policy of "peace with all nations, entangling alliances with none."[14] Many unionists saw increased armament production as protection against an "imaginary foe," an enemy that, in reality, did not exist.[15] The Miner's *Journal* again summed up the thinking of many when it declared that "there can be no danger of war unless we, by our actions, invite war."[16]

If, as President Wilson reiterated in speech after speech, there was no threat to our national security, the critics of preparedness within the labor movement began to seek other reasons for its advocacy. The causes were uncovered by those professing support of two different ideologies, often conflicting, often similar—the Marxian class struggle and economic determinism.

The conviction that the armed forces were merely tools in the hands of the wealthier classes was widely shared by the workingmen and their unions. The Railway Carmen voiced the opinion that since big business had fully exploited the domestic market, its support of preparedness was but the first and opening step in its campaign for world conquest.[17] In support of its thesis, the railwaymen quoted from a paper by Rear Admiral Chadwick to the effect that "Navies and armies are insurance for the wealth of the leisure class of a nation invested abroad."[18] The Minneapolis Trades and Labor Assembly and the Building Trades Council, which included practically all organized labor in the city, labeled the preparedness campaign as the work of a "few millionaires who arm the country," and whose private armies "at every opportunity have murdered and slain the workers."[19]

To a large number of trade unionists, the military were not impartial representatives of all the people but an instrument in the employ

14. *The Garment Worker* (September 10, 1915), p. 4.
15. *Ibid.; The Blacksmiths' Journal* 17 (December 1915): 10-12; *The Boilermakers' Journal* 26 (November 1914): 817-18.
16. *United Mine Workers' Journal* (June 17, 1915), p. 4.
17. *Railway Carmens' Journal* 21 (April 1916): 200-201.
18. *Ibid.*
19. *The Labor Review* (April 7, 1916), quoted in *New York Times*, June 3, 1916, p. 12.

of big business to be used for strikebreaking purposes.[20] Memories of the industrial battles of the past, of the union men and women killed by the military, of the Ludlows and the Calumets, were constantly rekindled in the union press as a reminder to the workingman of the dangers of an American rearmed.[21] Under its present method of organization, warned the Chicago Federation of Labor, a great army and navy "would be a powerful instrument for the conversion of the country into a commercial oligarchy."[22]

So strong was sentiment against the National Guard in the United Mine Workers, largest affiliate in the AFL, that some of the state locals passed laws forbidding its members to join that organization.[23] The president of the Miners, under pressure from the rank and file, evidently sought to pass a constitutional amendment barring a miner from joining the militia. However, upon the advice of legal counsel, the proposal was dropped.[24]

Labor's disenchantment with the armed forces had reached such a degree of bitterness as to be of major concern to those close to military establishment. Henry L. Stimson, former secretary of war in Taft's administration, recognized that the laboring classes regarded the soldiers not as their protector but as a "representative of capital being trained as a policeman against labor."[25] However, the purpose of Mr. Stimson's address had not been to give support to the opponents of preparedness, but to bring attention to the problem with the express purpose of assuaging labor's open hostility. To accomplish this end, Gompers, with the blessing of the Wilson Administration, was to devote his entire resources and energy.

In searching for the reasons behind preparedness, a vast number of labor leaders adopted the ideology of economic determinism and imputed economic motives to all demands for increased armament pro-

20. *The Tailor* (February 1, 1916); *United Mine Workers' Journal* (June 8, 1916), p. 9.
21. *Coast Seamen's Journal* (February 23, 1916); *The Blacksmiths' Journal* 17 (December 1915): 10-12.
22. *The Labor Herald* (June 2, 1916).
23. *The Tailor* (October 19, 1915).
24. Frank P. Walsh to John P. White, January 31, 1916, Frank P. Walsh Manuscripts, Manuscript Division, New York Public Library; John P. White to Walsh February 2, 1916, Walsh MSS.
25. Quoted in *Coast Seamen's Journal* (January 26, 1916).

duction. This attitude cut across diverse groups within the labor movement, and was the prevailing belief of the workingmen and their union leaders. They were convinced that preparedness was just a plot carefully woven by the munitions makers to increase their already-swollen profits.[26] In order to thwart the design of the munitions manufacturers, union opponents of preparedness proposed public ownership of all factories manufacturing arms and munitions, as well as control by the government of all natural resources and means of transportation that were connected with armament production.[27] While many of the unions in the present AFL-CIO may frown on such a socialist solution, union membership during the First World War accepted government control much more readily than their counterparts of today. Socialist sentiment was strong in the AFL and its advocacy was not dismissed lightly.

Gompers, politically shrewd and sensitively attuned to the thinking of his membership, sought to win support for Wilson's preparedness program by linking it not only with democratic reforms and procedures, but with mankind's basic aspirations for a better life. Following in the footsteps of Woodrow Wilson who, in his address before the opening session of the sixty-fourth Congress, linked preparedness to the development of the scientific, agricultural, industrial, and intellectual resources of the nation, Gompers redefined it as part of a larger problem of national development—physical, mental, economic and educational.[28] Military preparedness was to be "only a small segment of the general policy";[29] it was to be "but one of the phases of national life and not something separate" from it.[30] In essence, Gompers argued that if the workers were to accept military preparedness, the military could not ignore issues of human welfare.

26. *Cigar Makers' Official Journal* 39 (December 1915): 2; *The Fur Worker* (December 5, 1916); *United Mine Workers' Journal* (June 17, 1915); *Coast Seamen's Journal* (September 13, 1916).

27. *The Tailor* (October 5, 1915); *United Mine Workers' Journal* (September 23, 1915), p. 4; *Coast Seamen's Journal* (October 11, 1916); *The Labor Herald* (June 2, 1916).

28. Speech before the Sixteenth Annual Meeting of the National Civic Federation, January 18, 1916, in Samuel Gompers, *American Labor and the War* (New York: George H. Doran Company, 1919), pp. 57-58.

29. Gompers to Matthew Woll, May 8, 1916, Samuel Gompers Manuscripts, Manuscript Division, Library of Congress, Washington, D.C.

30. Gompers to Garrett Baxter, February (exact date unclear), 1916, Gompers MSS.

However, in his effort to make Wilson's program of self-defense more palatable to the workingman, he was to make of it something that it was not—a measure designed mainly to improve the educational and physical well-being of the nation. The result was that a national debate raged over the efficacy of military preparedness as an instrument to aid education and physical fitness. What was meant by "education" was soon to become apparent.

Gompers's response can best be seen by his support of the voluntary citizens' training camps later known as "the Plattsburgh idea." He cooperated with General Leonard Wood to establish such a camp for laboring men.[31] It was generally acknowledged that the camps had little value from a military point of view. General Wood, author of the idea and its leading protagonist, openly and candidly revealed that the true purpose of the camps was to serve as educational centers "to develop a proper and necessary appreciation of the duties and obligations of American citizenship" among the various racial and ethnic immigrant groups.[32] The personnel of the camps were to be trained to accept sound military values and to become an ideological army in leading the fight for military preparedness. Gompers raised no objections to such stated aims. Universal military service was, to him, simply another mode of education. Moreover, if the camps could "Americanize" the foreign born, the latter might be less susceptible to socialist preachings and more inclined to follow the AFL leadership. It was a case where the objectives of the military and the leadership of organized labor coalesced and joined forces.[33] Perhaps the most pungent and enlightening comment on the whole project was made by one of the leading educators of our time, John Dewey, who labeled the tendency to link military service with education "a deplorable self-deception."[34]

31. *New York Times*, September 25, 1915; Hermann Hagedorn, *Leonard Wood* (New York: Harper & Brothers, 1931), 2: 168; Millis, *Road to War*, p. 95.
32. Quoted in John Dewey, "Universal Service As Education," *The New Republic* (April 22, 1916), p. 309.
33. Frey to W. A. Appleton, May 20, 1919, Frey MSS. The AFL regarded the non-English-speaking elements as socialist oriented and a threat to their control of the trade-union movement.
34. *The New Republic* (April 22, 1916), p. 310. See also Randolph Bourne, "A Moral Equivalent for Universal Military Service," *The New Republic* (July 1, 1916), pp. 217-19.

When the secretary of war suggested that public school authorities introduce military training in the curriculum, it aroused some of the liveliest debates at every AFL convention during the war period. It resulted in one of those rare occasions when a recommendation by a committee to reject a resolution condemning the action of the secretary of war was overturned by the convention as a whole.[35] Gompers supported the government's position, reasoning that children lacked the "physical training [so essential] to make a virile manhood and womanhood."[36] He discounted the idea of militarism by placing his faith in the democracy of America.[37]

Gompers accepted the basic premise behind preparedness—the need of the nation to rearm in order to defend itself against a potential aggressor, namely Germany. His ideas ran somewhat parallel to those of the psychologist William James, in that he saw the causes of war rooted in man's pugnacious nature. This being the case, Gompers viewed rearmament as a necessary and deterrent factor and the best guarantor of peace.[38]

Yet, for Gompers to have attempted to lead the AFL into an open and forthright position in support of the military and its policies might well have brought about an open split in the Federation. The difficulty lay in the decades of mutually hostile relations between the two. As late as September 1915, the AFL leader was writing that army and navy officials went "out of their way to be antagonistic to the best interests of labor," particularly in situations where workers were engaged in union organization.[39] While this may not have proved to be an insuperable barrier for Gompers to cross in seeking an ideological alliance with high officials in the army and navy, as well as with their industrial counterparts, it was to prove a most dif-

35. AFL, *Proceedings* (1916), p. 310.
36. AFL, *Proceedings* (1915), p. 387.
37. For additional material on military training and the schools, see *The Bricklayer, Mason and Plasterer* 18 (August 1915): 171; AFL, *Proceedings* (1915), pp. 389-90; *The Tailor* (November 30, 1915); AFL, *Proceedings* (1916), pp. 303, 309-10; *The Survey* (December 2, 1916), p. 221; *Machinists' Monthly Journal* 29 (January 1917): 66; *American Federationist* 24 (January 1917): 30; *The Survey* (December 1, 1917), p. 232.
38. Gompers, *American Labor and the War*, p. 63; Gompers to T. Kitters Van Dyke, February 3, 1916, Gompers MSS; Gompers, "Why the War Was Not Prevented," *Harpers Weekly* (August 7, 1915), pp. 130-31.
39. Gompers to Honorable Scott Ferris, September 11, 1915, Gompers MSS.

ficult and burdensome obstacle in trying to lead workingmen to embrace preparedness doctrines.

In approaching the issue of national defense the AFL was forced to set up its own scale of priorities. Position or rank was to be determined by the Federation's conception of its own role in American society. Believing that labor could gain a foothold in American industry only through outright cooperation with the military, industry, and the government, Gompers sought to place preparedness as the top priority and objective before the labor movement. He therefore urged the workers to be guided by the interests of the nation as a whole and not just by labor's needs. Labor must rise above local pecuniary matters, he proclaimed, and adopt a "broad national viewpoint" in dealing with its problems[40] In answer to those who held that there were economic motives behind the preparedness drive, Gompers argued that it was not the responsibility of any one class but depended on the nation as a whole.

However, the national priorities established by the leadership of the AFL were not necessarily those adopted by the national unions. In the process of forming their own set of priorities, many union officials were, in effect, to undermine the Federation's support of the entire defense program as elaborated by the Wilson Administration. Typical was the attitude of Andrew Furuseth, president of the Sailor's Union, who declared that the foremost objective before the workers was the strengthening of their own union and that this was the only kind of preparedness over which they had a right to become enthusiastic.[41] In a similar vein, the Blacksmiths interpreted preparedness as a program to build their own organization against employer onslaughts in the coming years.[42] The president of the United Mine Workers saw as the first task before the workers the realization of all the American goals that up to that moment had been obtained only by the wealthy.[43]

An analysis of the attitude of the Machinists' Union is illuminating in that, on the one hand, it provides an excellent illustration of the

---

40. Gompers to E. J. Stock, May 16, 1916, Gompers MSS.
41. *Coast Seamen's Journal* (January 19, 1916).
42. *The Blacksmiths' Journal* 17 (September 1916): 10-11.
43. *United Mine Workers' Journal* (June 8, 1916), p. 9.

nature of the opposition to Gompers's sense of priorities, and, on the other, it explains why the opposition was not able to stem or divert the course followed by Gompers in the field of foreign policy. During 1915, opponents of Gompers's policies in the union adopted a posture of unconcern over military preparedness and sought to dwell only on those questions which were related to its affairs as a labor organization. They regarded the tremendous demand for machinists as giving the union an opportunity to meet the employers on an equal footing and to gain the long-sought-for eight-hour day, as well as other benefits.[44]

But the Machinists failed to take any role whatsoever in fighting against the Federation's flirtation with the proponents of rearmament. Its hands-off attitude only served to strengthen Gompers's policies within the AFL. What caused the Machinists Union to accept such an aloof and noncommital position? Part of the explanation appears to lie in the philosophy of nihilism that some of the union officials subscribed to. They condemned all governments and felt that to the workers it made little difference whether they were to be governed by the ruling class of Germany, England, France, or the United States.[45] The working class, wrote a general organizer of the union, should not concern itself with the "quarrels of the bankers and the manufacturers. . . . If the masters of this country want preparedness, let them go to war and protect their credits; but let the working class protect their unions. . . ."[46] The effect of such thinking was, by default, to accelerate the trend to military preparedness. It isolated the union from any role in the formulation of foreign policy and strengthened the prevalent attitude of leaving all affairs outside the union to "Sam."

Neither Gompers nor any other official of organized labor could publicly proclaim its support of the army and navy without, at the same time, seeking guarantees that the military would institute democratic reforms, and not be used, as in the past, as a weapon against labor. Preparedness to Gompers was not to be confused with militarism, the latter being vanquished by a thorough democratization

44. *Machinists' Monthly Journal* 28 (January 1916): 6-7, 94-95.
45. *Ibid.* 27 (February 1916): 171-72.
46. *Ibid.*

of the military system. This, according to the Federation leader, was to be accomplished by making military training voluntary and as general as possible. All naval and military schools were to be open to anyone who desired to enter.[47] Equal opportunities were to exist for all and no special professional distinctions among personnel were to be made that were based on special opportunities available only to a few.[48] Combined with the fact that the commander-in-chief of the army and navy was an elected official, such a program seemed, to Gompers, to constitute a significant precaution against militarism.[49]

Of prime importance to the AFL chief was that labor be represented on all agencies involved with the nation's self-defense.[50] He saw this as a means not only to make preparedness more effective,[51] but as an additional safeguard against the military misuse and abuse of power. Besides, Gompers surmised, such a move would grant to labor coequal status with other interests and establish it as a necessary and vital partner in the American economic system.

Imbued with his own sense of priorities, Gompers early went on record in support of measures that would enhance the position of the armed forces. At the 1915 Convention, the executive council gave its stamp of approval to the Dick Military Law, a measure enacted in 1903 to promote the efficiency of the militia.[52] When pacifist Amos Pinchot asked the AFL to take a position against increased subsidies for the National Guard, he "was turned down cold."[53]

Yet, labor remained uneasy. Many sought concrete assurances from the Federation chief that his program of democratization of the army would be carried out and that the latter never again could be used as an instrument against the labor movement. In his replies,

47. Gompers to General Leonard Wood, September 15, 1915, Woodrow Wilson Manuscripts, Manuscript Division, Library of Congress, Washington, D.C.
48. *Ibid.*
49. *Ibid.*
50. Gompers to Henry L. West, January 19, 1916, Gompers MSS: *American Federationist* 23 (February 1916): 105-10; Gompers, *American Labor and the War,* p. 63.
51. Gompers to Michael Goldsmith, February 29, 1916, National Civic Federation Manuscripts, Manuscript Division, New York Public Library.
52. AFL, *Proceedings* (1915), pp. 86-88.
53. Amos Pinchot to Members of the Committee of the American Union Against Militarism, May 20, 1916, Amos Pinchot Manuscripts, Manuscript Division, Library of Congress, Washington, D.C.

Gompers essentially placed his entire reliance not on concrete guarantees supplied by the Wilson Administration or high officials in the army and navy, but on vague political abstractions and faith. Answering charges that the Dick Military Law might be used against workers, Gompers replied that the best safeguard against misuse of the law was the assertion by workers of their civic rights.[54] The electoral process was, in effect, the best guarantee Gompers had to offer. Furthermore, Gompers assured his labor constituency, even among the capitalist class, he had heard the "expression that the military must not be used as strikebreaking agencies in the interest of employers."[55] To those who would link preparedness with militarism, Gompers would write that he knew "of no one who has brought out, or even holds in reserve, the idea of militarism."[56] In the end, as was to be the case in most matters concerning national defense and foreign policy, Gompers would lead the Federation into outright support of the preparedness program, but his promises of a reformed and restructured military machine were never to be realized.

However, Gompers's support of preparedness did bear fruit. He was responsibile for influencing many union officials to withdraw their support from the various peace groups. National unions also began to shift their position. The Cigar Makers represent a case in point. Prior to Gompers's public support of preparedness, the union regarded peace propaganda as subversive only to "the plutocrats . . . [and] profit mongers in war materials."[57] Immediately after Gompers's address, the Cigar Makers changed their tune, wrote of preparedness as preordained and inevitable, and saw the only issue before the labor movement as its right to "have some voice in the kind, quality and quantity it [should] be."[58] By May of 1916, the union had executed a full turn, and in a pleading tone asserted that the trade unions were the best means to prepare citizens to become good soldiers.[59] The reason: "the unions gave men something to

54. AFL, *Weekly News Letter* (January 1, 1916); AFL, *Proceedings* (1915), pp. 86-88.
55. AFL, *Proceedings* (1915), p. 388.
56. Gompers to C. W. Bowerman, January 25, 1916, Gompers MSS.
57. *Cigar Makers' Official Journal* 39 (December 1915): 2.
58. *Ibid.* 40 (February 1916): 2.
59. *Ibid.* 40 (May 1916): 2

fight for. Men will therefore not be inclined to say 'Why Should I Fight?' "[60] Essentially, the union was willing to exchange its support and participation in the foreign-policy objectives of the nation for the recognition of labor as a legitimate factor in American life.

If some unions wavered under the relentless pressure to conform, many did not. Opposition to preparedness continued to flourish. By June of 1916, *The New Republic* reported that many labor circles regarded the mobilization of United States war strength with a "cold indifference."[61] An Eastern-state labor leader who took an unofficial poll of the state and local labor unions throughout the country revealed that the results indicated practically unanimous opposition to any plan to enlarge significantly the standing army or to increase army or navy expenditures.[62]

The *Cleveland Citizen* informed its readers that an overwhelming majority of the membership—4,432 to 565, or about one-half of the local unions affiliated with the Cleveland Federation of Labor—voted to condemn all military preparations being promoted by the statesmen in the nation's capital.[63] *The Labor Clarion* of San Francisco, the Spokane *Labor Herald,* and the Allentown *Labor Herald,* all labor journals, continued to oppose preparedness as a measure designed to involve the country in the European war.[64]

James Lord, president of the Mine Department of the AFL, admitted that preparedness programs left the average workingman "cold and sullen. There is something fundamental in all these military schemes," reported Lord, "for which he [the worker] simply cannot stand."[65] On the eve of the presidential election, the California State Federation of Labor voiced its "unalterable opposition to all forms of military preparedness."[66]

Many of the unions, despite appeals to their patriotism, refused to take part in any of the Preparedness Day parades. The Sailors' Union of the Pacific repudiated the parades as artificial stimulants to arouse

60. *Ibid.*
61. *The New Republic* (June 10, 1916), pp. 137-39.
62. *Ibid.*
63. Cited by *The Literary Digest* (April 8, 1916), p. 957.
64. *Ibid.,* p. 958.
65. *St. Louis Post-Dispatch,* March 11, 1916, quoted in *National Rip Saw* (May 1916), p. 12.
66. *Coast Seamen's Journal* (October 11, 1916).

patriotism and urged its members to refrain from participation.[67] The Waterfront Workers Federation of San Francisco, as well as the Central Labor Councils of Seattle, Washington, and Portland, Oregon, quickly followed suit.[68] The United Mine Workers complained that workers were being forced to march in the parades and threatened with loss of their jobs if they refused to do so. To the Miners, the main danger to the workers was "from within the State and not without."[69] The Industrial Council of Kansas City supported the Miners' contention.[70] As the summer of 1916 approached, the president of the San Francisco Labor Council, Daniel C. Murphy, could report that not one central labor council nor a single labor union had been officially represented in a Preparedness Day parade.[71]

As 1916 drew to a close, working-class opposition to all military measures, although its ranks were somewhat slimmer, remained militant and strong. It was ideologically fueled by the belief of the working men that they had little stake in the American economic system, that the national quarrels were not of their own making, and that the main battle for them was that of the poor against the rich.[72] Try as he might, Gompers could not shake the workers from this conviction.

What was remarkable about the dissent in the American Federation of Labor was its tenacity and broad scope and depth, which enabled it to withstand all the organizational pressures Gompers could bring to bear, as well as the power and persuasiveness of the Administration in Washington. Opposition to President Wilson's defense policies was to continue up to the very moment the United States entered the war.

67. *Ibid.* (May 24, 1916).
68. *Ibid.* (May 31, 1916).
69. *United Mine Workers' Journal* (June 15, 1916), p. 4.
70. *The Labor Herald* (June 16, 1916).
71. *Coast Seaman's Journal* (July 26, 1916).
72. *New York Times,* December 25, 1916, p. 3.

5
Labor's Declaration of War

Within six months after his reelection as president on a platform of "He Kept Us Out of War," and within a month after his inauguration, Woodrow Wilson went before the Congress and asked for a declaration of war against Germany. Wilson, with a rhetorical flourish beyond compare, painted a glowingly democratic portrait of America's war aims and objectives. It was to be a war to make the world "safe for democracy." We had "no selfish ends to serve," and we had entered the war, Wilson stressed, only because "the right is more precious than peace."

While historians have long debated the wisdom of Wilson's grandiloquent rhetoric, its usage was, in part, dictated by practical necessities. It was meant to build an ideological bridge between the government's acts and the American people—the vast majority of whom gave little sign that they were willing or enthusiastic about joining the Allied powers in the European conflict. While it is difficult to employ an accurate gauge to measure feeling at the time, it was clear that opposition to the war was very broad and deep. No national demand existed for Wilson to take the country into war.[1] Quite the contrary; if the majority accepted the president's war resolution because no other alternative seemed possible, millions of

1. Arthur S. Link, *Wilson, Campaigns For Progressivism and Peace, 1916-1917* (Princeton: Princeton University Press, 1965), 5:411, 429.

Americans were still convinced that intervention was the design of evil forces, which saw involvement in the war as beneficial to their own interests.[2] This attitude even permeated the halls of Congress where Senator Norris, on the eve of war, voiced the sentiment of many when he declared: "We are going into war upon the command of gold. . . .We are about to put the dollar sign upon the American flag."[3]

Wilson was cognizant of the divisions among the American people and recognized that his policies in foreign affairs could be successful only if they were supported by a united country.[4] Opposition to the war had reached such proportions that upon our entrance into the conflict, the president's "chief preoccupation" was with the ever-present danger of civil discord.[5]

One of the main roadblocks hampering the unity of the American people was the polyglot nature of the population. America was a conglomerate mass of different nationalities, with each group tied ethnically, culturally, and emotionally to the homeland of its birth.

It was among the immigrant ethnic groups that Gompers sought to play a decisive role. After all, the American Federation of Labor was the "home" of large numbers of German, Irish, and Jewish citizens, whose antagonism to the Allies often bordered on violence. It was Gompers's task to integrate United States aims and objectives overseas with the interests of the workingman so as to minimize the opposition of these groups to American involvement in the European conflict. The president of the AFL aimed to weld the hyphenated Americans into a solid phalanx in support of Wilson's program.

On February 3, 1917, Woodrow Wilson broke off diplomatic relations with Germany. This was the signal for many advocates of

2. Arthur S. Link, *American Epoch* (New York: Alfred A. Knopf, 1955), p. 208; Arno J. Mayer, *Political Origins of the New Diplomacy, 1917-1918* (New Haven: Yale University Press, 1959), p. 347; Louis Filler, *Randolph Bourne* (Washington D. C.: American Council on Public Affairs, 1943), pp. 89-90.
3. George W. Norris, *Fighting Liberal* (New York: The Macmillan Company, 1945), pp. 196-97. See also Eric F. Goldman, *Rendezvous With Destiny* (New York: Alfred A. Knopf, 1952), pp. 238-42.
4. John L. Heaton, *Cobb of "The World"* (New York: E. P. Dutton & Company, 1924), p. 219.
5. Ray Stannard Baker, *Woodrow Wilson: Life and Letters* (Garden City, N.Y.: Doubleday, Doran and Company, 1939), 7: 447-49.

peace to spring into action. The response from labor was not all that Gompers desired. Trade-union opposition to any war with the Central Powers was widespread.

In order to blunt the war momentum, the forces for peace raised a fundamentally democratic issue that was designed to have wide appeal among a democratically minded people. They demanded, in effect, that war could be declared only if a referendum vote of all the American people sanctioned such a course of action. Thus, Congress would be effectively robbed of this power. Many in the labor movement identified with this view. The Industrial Council of Kansas City gave it its wholehearted endorsement.[6] James H. Maurer, president of the Pennsylvania State Federation of Labor, asked labor to declare a general strike if the government refused to grant a referendum vote on any declaration of war.[7] A committee consisting of the United Hebrew Trades, the International Clothing Workers' Union, Amalgamated Clothing Workers' Union, and other labor groups organized a Keep Out of War Committee to support the demand for a war referendum.[8]

Powerfully articulated and having at its core a basic democratic quality, the demand for a referendum was upsetting to Gompers's libertarian equanimity. He tactically sought to sidetrack the issue. However, the charge that the United States entered the war without the voluntary consent of its people, and that it was aided and abetted in this procedure by the AFL, brought forth constant rejoinders from Gompers as to the democratic practices in American life. He could never let the issue rest. Months after our declaration of war against Germany he was defending his anti-referendum position on constitutional grounds.[9]

Labor's anti-war partisans would not be silenced. The Painters' Union challenged some of the basic assumptions feeding the demand for war: national honor, dignity, freedom of the seas, and protection of peaceful citizens. All these, the union held, could be assured

6. *The Labor Herald* (February 16, 1917).
7. *New York Times,* February 5, 1917, p. 2.
8. *Ibid.*
9. Speech before Anti-Disloyalty Mass Meeting, November 2, 1917, in Samuel Gompers, *American Labor and the War* (New York: George H. Doran Co., 1919), p. 135.

without making war on Germany.[10] Furthermore, it was the opinion of the union that the crisis was engendered by the war traders and financiers who wanted to control the world's market and exploit the workers.[11] Joining with advocates of a referendum, the Painters held to the position that Congress would be unjustified in declaring war without the American people's having expressed themselves on the subject.[12] In Toledo, Ohio, 2,500 members of the Machinists' Union favored calling a general strike if the government refused to heed the people's demand for peace.[13]

On the West Coast, a center of anti-war sentiment, the Sailor's Union was organizing a campaign to send letters and telegrams to the president expressing the feeling of its members that the workers had "no reason . . . to shed their blood for the protection and furtherance of the unholy profits of their masters. . . ."[14] The Saint Louis Central Trades Council unanimously adopted a resolution appealing to the president and Congress "to do all in their power to keep the United States out of war."[15]

Socialistically inclined and with a large German membership, the Bakers' Union protested vociferously against the possibility of United States participation in the European struggle. Our entry, warned the union, would serve only to "perpetuate capitalism."[16]

The largest and strongest central body in the country, the Chicago Federation of Labor, adopted a resolution demanding that the country not be dragged into the European holocaust.[17] The Cigar Makers also voiced their dissent to being dragged into the war.[18] In Joplin, Missouri, the Trade Assembly could find no "excuse or reason" for the war in Europe or for any war that ever existed.[19] It sought a peaceful solution through the introduction of a new diplomacy.

If Gompers saw the war as sparking the rebirth of the labor

10. *The Painter and Decorator* 31 (February 1917): 83-84.
11. *Ibid.*
12. *Ibid.*
13. *Coast Seamen's Journal* (March 28, 1917).
14. *Ibid.* (February 21, 1917).
15. *American Socialist* (March 24, 1917).
16. *The Bakers' Journal* (February 10, 1917), p. 1.
17. *Ibid.* (February 17, 1917), p. 2.
18. *Cigar Makers' Official Journal* 41 (February 1917): 2.
19. *Railway Carmen's Journal* 22 (February 1917): 70.

movement, the president of the Teamsters, taking a different tack, viewed it as a potential disaster. Tobin, echoing Wilson's concern, saw all union rules and gains achieved by the workers being sacrificed upon the altar of war's needs.[20] He urged the membership to maintain their standards and to be prepared to fight for the very existence of the organization.[21] Thus, unlike Gompers, peace, to the Teamsters, was a vital ingredient for the growth and development of the trade unions.

What was the sentiment of the trade unions on the eve of war? When the Central Federated Union of New York City called upon President Wilson "to resist the selfish and sinister influences that would plunge our country into the world cauldron of murder," the *New Republic* gauged this expression as typical of the feeling of union men and women.[22] This analysis is of particular importance when we consider that the policies of the magazine at that time were shaped largely by those who were close to or played a part in the Wilson Administration.

While opposition to the war was escalating among the union membership, Gompers was overly anxious to prove labor's loyalty to the Administration's foreign policies. He measured patriotism by the degree of one's support of these policies. Central to Gompers's thought was the conception that qualitative changes were in the making in the industrial and governmental sectors of American society, and for labor to participate in and affect these changes—to be, in a sense, a partner in the revamping of society—labor must first prove its loyalty and fidelity to the nation and its institutions. He therefore never tired of gathering an audience to which he might extol the patriotic virtues of the AFL. In order to secure labor support, he tied patriotism and the welfare of the workers in the same bundle and made each dependent on the other. When the House of Representatives was considering repealing the Eight Hour Law of 1892 as a measure necessitated by the war crisis, Gompers wrote the Speaker, Champ Clark, assuring him that in the event of war organized workers would "give a

20. *Official Magazine—Teamsters* 14 (April 1917): 4-5.
21. *Ibid.*
22. *The New Republic* (February 10, 1917), pp. 38-40.

good accounting of themselves."[23] In reply, the Speaker stated that he felt confident that repeal would be unnecessary since he knew that, if needed, labor would work sixteen hours a day.[24] Gompers did not demur but cited this as proof of the effectiveness of his position.

Gompers's rapport with the Wilson Administration frequently led him to boast that labor received greater consideration in the United States from the Government than that accorded to any labor movement by any Government elsewhere in the world.[25] Yet, nagging questions always seemed to arise to place in doubt the benefits to the workingman of this special relationship. For example, in the midst of the war-induced prosperity of February 1917, the Machinists were focusing their attention on the "long bread lines" and the "food riots" that were occurring with ever-greater frequency.[26] The union desired government action to halt the profiteering in food, but saw this as providing only temporary relief. Its final solution lay in "Government control of the means of production and distribution."[27]

Support of Wilson's foreign policies during the few months preceding the declaration of war also led the Federation into a position where it sought to keep labor quiet and docile, since any strike or industrial disturbance was widely regarded as unpatriotic and weakening the country's position during a period of crisis. In March, the Railroad Brotherhoods threatened to strike over the eight-hour day. Instantaneously, the president of the Union Pacific charged that the threatened strike was the work of foreign elements that sought to embarrass the nation at a critical time.[28] Wilson appointed a committee, of which Gompers was a member, to attempt to settle the dispute. The Federation made no concerted effort to rally organized labor behind the Brotherhoods. Instead, it was widely reported that the president of the AFL did not approve of the Brotherhoods' push-

23. Gompers to Champ Clark, February 4, 1917, cited in AFL, *Proceedings* (1917), pp. 107-8. See also Gompers to Executive Council, February 10, 1917, Gompers MSS.
24. Champ Clark to Gompers, February 6, 1917, cited in AFL, *Proceedings* (1917), pp. 107-8.
25. *Coast Seamen's Journal* (February 21, 1917).
26. *Machinists' Monthly Journal* 29 (March 1917): 266-67.
27. *Ibid.*
28. *New York Times,* March 17, 1917, p. 1.

ing for an eight-hour day at such a crucial period in the nation's history.[29] It was to be one of the many acts of "statesmanship" by Gompers. He was later to be acclaimed as a great patriot who put the nation's interest first and labor's second.

Gompers's eagerness to portray labor in a patriotic light eventually led some unions willingly to surrender gains labor had won at the cost of great sacrifice. On March 28, the New York State Federation of Labor, imbued with the spirit of patriotism, approved, without being requested to do so, the suspension of statutes enacted by the state to safeguard the workers, including women and children.[30] So happy was the State Assembly to comply that within a few days it had prepared a bill to eliminate all restrictions upon the employment of men as well as upon the night work of women and children.[31] A storm of protest forced the State Federation to rescind its stand, but it was a prelude to the kind of position the AFL would take in the coming years.

Gompers was now faced with a dual problem. He was extraordinarily anxious to prove, in no uncertain terms, organized labor's loyalty and patriotism, and, in order to accomplish this goal, he was desirous finally and irrevocably to commit the AFL to Wilson's war policies in the face of growing peace sentiment among the unions. It was decided by the Federation president that this could best be achieved by calling a conference of all AFL unions together with the Railroad Brotherhoods to articulate labor's position during the war crisis. The meeting was held on March 12 at AFL headquarters in Washington, D.C.

It has generally been accepted that the Conference was called on Gompers's initiative. However, evidence now indicates the possibility that Gompers had reacted to governmental pressure. On the day after the Conference, the *New York Times* reported that the meeting was held at the suggestion of the Council of National Defense.[32] This was subsequently confirmed by a labor journalist close to AFL headquarters in Washington, D.C.—Lawrence Todd.[33] The fact that

29. *Ibid.*
30. *The New Republic* (April 14, 1917), pp. 312-13.
31. *Ibid.*
32. *New York Times*, March 13, 1917, p. 1.
33. *Coast Seamen's Journal* (March 28, 1917).

Gompers inquired as to the feasibility of the Government's paying the expense of calling so many labor officials to Washington—the matter was to be discussed at the next meeting of the Advisory Commission of the Council of National Defense—lays open to question the assertion that the Conference was a deliberative body called together for the express purpose of formulating labor's position on peace and war.[34] It also raises the question whether any meeting financed by government sources can actually arrive at a position that might be at variance with government policy.

With these facts in mind, doubt arises as to what the Conference document really represented. Was it reflective of the actual feelings of an overwhelming majority of trade unionists, or was it a document favored only by certain sectors of organized labor and brought into fruition by a combination of parliamentary maneuvering and shrewd usage of internal and external pressures? In light of the proceedings of the Conference, the criticisms raised by some of the leading participants, and the degree of government involvement, it would be accurate to interpret the Conference of March 12 as the result of a collusive arrangement between leaders of the AFL and elements in the Wilson Administration for the specific purposes of stemming the growing tide of opposition to a foreign policy that might involve the United States in the European conflict and, at the same time, solidly aligning labor with any policy pursued by the Administration in Washington.

The document brought forth by the Conference was noteworthy for the manner in which it gave blanket approval to whatever steps Wilson might take in the field of foreign relations. The Federation made its wholehearted support subject to three provisos: recognition by the government of organized labor as the agency with which it must cooperate in its dealings with wage earners; the granting to workers of a direct voice in the establishment and implementation of public policy affecting industry; and representation of labor on all bodies dealing with national defense.[35]

---

34. Franklin H. Martin, *Digest of the Proceedings of the Council of National Defense During the War* (Washington, D.C.: United States Government Printing Office, 1934), pp. 101-2.
35. The composition of the March 12 Conference and its declaration may be found in AFL, *Proceedings* (1917), pp. 72-78.

Gompers often pointed with pride to the fact that all decisions reached at the meeting were by unanimous vote. In fact, the entire document as drawn up by the Executive Council on March 9 was accepted intact without a single alteration. Yet, this was in no way indicative of what really went on inside the conference hall. Gompers deliberately sought to create the impression of unanimity, but the declaration was not approved without a bitter struggle, led by some of the leading figures in the trade union movement.[36]

Perhaps the most caustic critic of the entire conference was the president of the Teamsters, Daniel Tobin, who was reported by the newspapers to have filibustered against adoption of the declaration.[37] Tobin was critical of the entire procedure employed at the conference. Expecting to consult and advise with the Executive Council on the formulation of policy, Tobin was chagrined to find that the document had already been prepared and that he was expected to approve of it as a matter of formality.[38] When Tobin asked that the entire matter be referred back to the international unions for endorsement, since those present had no sanction from their membership to commit their union, he was turned down.[39] Even his proposal to delay action until the following morning was refused.[40] Tobin concluded that "there was really no need of calling the representatives of Labor to Washington. . .when there was a cut and dried program already prepared which might have been mailed to the International Officers. . . ."[41]

Andrew Furuseth of the Sailors' Union characterized the document as a virtual declaration of war and afterwards stated to Gompers: "That sounds the death-knell of the A. F. of L., and your forty years of work for labor you have destroyed today."[42]

The Amalgamated Clothing Workers, which was not affiliated with the AFL and hence not a participant at the conference, agreed with Tobin that the meeting was not representative of the thinking of the

36. Gompers to James Duncan, March 23, 1917, Gompers MSS.
37. *New York Times,* March 13, 1917, p. 1.
38. *Official Magazine—Teamsters* 14 (April 1917): 9-11.
39. *Ibid.*
40. *Ibid.*
41. *Ibid.*
42. AFL, *Proceedings* (1919), p. 412.

membership since apparently not a single union had its members ratify its action at the conference.[43] Max Hayes of the Miners regarded the results as a foregone conclusion, one that was imposed and not the product of a deliberative body.[44]

A curious anomaly was presented by the action of the Fur Workers and the Journeyman Tailors. Both unions expressed themselves in militant socialist terms and both were vociferously opposed to the war. They reacted in a similar manner at the conference, but in a dissimilar manner after the event. The position of the Fur Workers is striking in that it provides some understanding of voting patterns at the March 12 conference. Its president attended the conference but failed to vote officially against the declaration. Notwithstanding, the union continued its bitter opposition to United States participation in the war, and in its journal noted that its opinion was at variance with the declaration produced by the conference.[45]

On the other hand, the Journeyman Tailors, ideologically sympathetic to the Fur Workers and second to none in its socialist outlook, showed the effects of the conference by comparing its declaration with the Ten Commandments.[46] Hereafter, its official publication avoided all mention of foreign policy issues and concentrated solely on domestic affairs. Its opposition to the war had become muted.

Thus the position of the Furriers at the conference and afterwards was similar to that of Tobin of the Teamsters, Furuseth of the Sailors, and delegates from the Painters and Miners Union. None wished to be recorded as voting against the declaration, yet, after the conference, each either directly and openly denounced its results or actively worked for a position contrary to it. The question naturally arises as to why these delegates did not exercise their option and vote against the conference declaration. The answer probably lies in fear—fear of exposing their minority position before a hostile public opinion, and of making their union subject to the displeasure and enmity of the government as well as the Gompers forces that controlled the machinery of the AFL.

43. *Advance* (April 13, 1917), p. 4.
44. *American Socialist* (March 24, 1917).
45. *The Fur Worker* (April 3, 1917).
46. *The Tailor* (March 27, 1917).

It would be extremely unfair to label these men as lacking in courage. The trade unions of 1917 cannot be compared with their counterparts of today. They were constantly in a virtual life-and-death struggle for existence and did not always enjoy the luxury of voting according to their conscience. A union's survival was inextricably tied to its ability to obtain the help and cooperation of fellow unionists. Organizational campaigns in the smaller towns could succeed only through the joint efforts of the AFL and officials of other unions. Combined with the fact that government assistance could be a crucial factor in the determination of negotiations or in a strike, the expression of dissent could become a hazardous undertaking for many unions. The forces of power made for compliance.

Some of Gompers's opponents eventually reversed themselves and came to accept his position as the correct one. However, many reached this conclusion not by examining the merits of Gompers's policies, but on purely pragmatic grounds. For example, the Trades and Labor Assembly of Minneapolis, a peace advocate, upon reflection and reexamination of its position, came to recognize that Gompers's achievements lay in his ability to ascertain that war was inevitable, and, by refusing to join a losing cause, Gompers was able to adopt policies best suited to protect the Federation.[47]

Despite opposition, the declaration did have the effect of aligning the labor movement behind the president's foreign policies. It officially committed organized labor to a specific program and made it extremely difficult for its opponents openly to oppose it. It guaranteed that the workingmen, particularly the ethnic groups of German, Irish, and Jewish descent, would not have the support of the Federation if they undertook concerted action to thwart its wishes. It made the welfare of the workers and the unions dependent on their wholehearted cooperation with the Administration's war policies. And, above all, it isolated the peace groups from the trade-union movement, and cast them in the villainous role of being traitors to the unions and the workers if they continued their anti-war crusade.

Gompers viewed the conference as having an enormous impact on

---

47. AFL, *Weekly News Letter* (April 21, 1917).

the labor movement as well as on Wilson's thinking. He was firmly convinced that the declaration of March 12 had helped to dispel some of the fears of the president, who had many misgivings about the unity of the people, particularly the various ethnic groups, should the United States undertake active participation in the European conflict. The conference, he felt, made possible Wilson's address before Congress in which he asked for a declaration of war against Germany.[48]

But, if Gompers was convinced that labor's declaration of fidelity to the Administration's objectives was of great aid in aligning the forces of democracy and justice against autocracy and militarism, he also entertained the thought that organized labor had, at the same time, furthered its own interests. From the moment of the signing of the March 12 document, Gompers asserted, there had "not been a difference of opinion between the policy of the Government of the United States and of the organized bodies of the working people."[49] This was the key to Gompers's understanding of what he regarded as profound and qualitative changes taking place in American society. Changes brought about by the very nature of the war were viewed by the AFL leader not as temporary or crisis produced, but as reflecting new growth and basic changes in the process of historical industrial development. Labor's position of March 12 was seen as bringing into being a new force in world economics and politics—a "fifth estate"—which was to have an equal share with the other estates in the decision-making process.[50] It was the beginning, in the view of the AFL Executive Council led by Gompers, of the transformation of the state from an organ that oppressed the workingman into one that became vitally concerned with his well-being. In a word, they saw the incipient growth of what has now matured into, and been labeled the "welfare state," and ascribed to it the bringing forth of a new utopia for labor.[51]

48. AFL, *Proceedings* (1919), p. 5; Samuel Gompers, *Seventy Years of Life and Labor* (New York: E. P. Dutton and Company, 1925), 2: 378; idem, *American Labor and the War,* pp. 230, 233, 241, 288.
49. Speech in Canadian House of Commons, April 26, 1918, in Gompers, *American Labor and the War,* p. 203. See also Gompers, *Seventy Years* 2: 359
50. Chester M. Wright, "Fifth Estate Becomes A World Power," *Machinist's Monthly Journal* 29 (April 1917): 389-91. The author was former editor of the *New York Call* and a pro-war Socialist who left the party because of its anti-war stand. During the period of the war he worked closely with Gompers and his opinions often reflected the thinking of the Federation leadership.
51. *Ibid.*

With labor patriotically behind the governmental process —Gompers was appointed a member of the Advisory Commission of the Council of National Defense—the Federation began to see the possibility of the "beginning of the merging of labor and state."[52] For Gompers and his followers this was to have profound consequences. They saw the struggle for labor conditions as no longer a matter of only private concern, but one in which the public, or state, was to play a major role.[53] As the "fifth estate," the Federation leaders saw themselves as direct participants in the determination of working conditions. To the AFL this was the beginning of industrial democracy. The Federation leaders were concerned lest some in the labor movement thwart this trend by refusing to cooperate with President Wilson and the business community in furtherance of the nation's policies abroad. This was the ideological core behind the AFL's unstinting support of Wilson's foreign policies and its willingness to enter the war against Germany.

52. *Ibid.*
53. *Ibid.*

6

Government and Labor —Partners in Industrial Mobilization

On April 6, 1917, after days of stormy and acrimonious debate, the political leaders of the country reached the decision that the interests of the nation necessitated a declaration of war against Germany. Once the political decision had been made, the United States began to prepare its vast industrial and military machine to meet the demands of war. It was not to be an easy task.

The First World War was witness to the drastic changes that had occurred in the methods of waging modern war. Armies in the field were no longer the sole determinants of victory or defeat. The organization of a nation's industrial plant, the proper utilization of its natural resources and manpower, and the morale of its people had become necessary, if not vital factors, in the world-wide conflict that now emerged. The army of working men in the factories was fully as important to the nation's military success as the soldiers who were manning the front lines. Although important elements in the military and industrial establishment resisted such a conclusion, it was wholeheartedly accepted by Wilson and Gompers.[1] Their cooperation and close working relationship were based on their recognition that labor and its relations to industry and government would be a central factor in winning the war.

Wilson's concern for industrial relations was well-founded. The experiences of the English and French during the first two years of the war firmly brought home the lesson that without organized labor's enthusiastic support, victory in the worldwide conflict was problematical. Through his deference and concessions to the AFL in problems involving labor relations, the president sought to construct his foreign policy upon a firm pillar of labor support.

If Wilson's objectives were obvious, Gompers's, in comparison, were more obscure. It was to be expected that the president of the AFL, an ardent practitioner of business unionism, would use organized labor's greatly improved bargaining position during the war to secure more bread for labor's table. Such was not to be the case. Collective bargaining was subordinated to the nation's wartime needs. The objectives of Wilson's foreign policies became the Federation's primary aim, the needs of the workingman secondary in relation to the nation's lofty goal of making the world "safe for democracy." Thus, AFL policy became that of securing benefits to its members only to the extent necessary to prevent interruption of production.

In a true sense, Gompers's view of labor relations was predicated on his belief that the worldwide objectives of the United States heralded a new era for labor. Labor must sacrifice, Gompers held, to show that it was patriotic and responsible and, as such, deserving of a share of power in the state. Collective bargaining thus became a weapon in the hands of the AFL hierarchy, not as a means for "more, more" benefits for the workingman, but as an instrument to ingratiate organized labor with the ruling powers in industry and government. It was to be a means of proving labor's total and un-

1. Speech before Annual Meeting of National Civic Federation, January 18, 1916, in Samuel Gompers, *American Labor and the War* (New York: George H. Doran Company, 1919), p. 55. Gompers, *American Labor and the War*, p. 55; *American Federationist* 25 (October 1918): 918-19; Grosvenor B. Clarkson, *Industrial America in the World War* (Boston and New York: Houghton Mifflin Company, 1924), p. 12.

flinching support of the foreign-policy goals as outlined by the Wilson Administration. Thus foreign policy and industrial relations were inextricably woven together, neither being capable of being understood without the other.

Gompers's policy in support of the war and its concomitant labor program which, in effect, placed a ceiling on the worker's ability to advance his standard of living, was bound to arouse intense opposition. Dissent to AFL policies centered in two groups: ideologically oriented pacifists, socialists, and trade unionists who disagreed with the Federation's support of United States intervention in the European conflict; and those labor men, both conservative and liberal, who strongly objected to subordinating the needs of the union as well as the conditions of the workers to the exigencies of war. Each caused deep concern among the Federation leadership and the Wilson Administration. So interrelated was the peace movement with the striving of workers for greater economic gain that an attack on one proved to be an attack on both.

Dissatisfaction with Gompers's policies among the workers grew to such proportions as to threaten to undermine his influence within the Federation and destroy forever the illusion that the workers accepted Gompers's "statesmanlike" approach to the world crisis. The history of labor during the war was a story of continual strife, struggle, and upheaval, resulting in an unprecedented number of strikes and bursting forth as the number-one problem before the Government. But to no other man, not even excluding President Wilson, goes the credit for being able to channel this dissent within tolerable limits.

Nearly two years before American participation in the war, Gompers had already begun to organize the industrial machinery and manpower of the country for its eventual conversion to wartime use. Plans for industrial mobilization in the event of war were quietly being laid in 1915. The Industrial Preparedness Committee, a part of the Naval Consulting Board, was formed to study the ability of industry to meet the requirements of the military in case of war. In charge of the project was a noted industrialist, Howard Coffin.

Gompers was introduced to the work of the Committee by Ralph Easley of the NCF, a firm supporter of military preparedness. The president of the Federation gave Coffin an excellent example of his devotion to the cause of national self-defense by working indefatigably to produce concrete results. A list was prepared detailing the capacity of industry to convert to the manufacture of munitions. Gompers was later to claim that this saved the United States six months' time when it entered the war.[2]

Gompers's unofficial work for the Industrial Preparedness Committee was soon superseded by his being officially chosen as a full-fledged partner of the government's defense program. The Military Appropriations Act of 1916 contained a provision creating a civilian agency for the purpose of studying the physical and human resources of the country in order to "make the calling out and mobilizing of the industrial resources of the nation as automatic as the mobilization of the army."[3] It was to coordinate industrial production with military needs. The new body, named by the Senate as the Council of National Defense, was to consist of the secretaries of war, navy, commerce, agriculture, labor, and the interior. Provision was also made for an advisory commission of seven members to be appointed by the president for the purpose of assisting the Council.

It was the beginning of an agency that was to take major responsibility for organizing the economic system to cope with the demands of war. Very little publicity was given to its formation, the Wilson Administration not desiring to rouse the ire of the pacifists, who were sure to see in its creation a step toward war.

As far back as 1910, military men had begun to ponder the idea of a CND. Some, like General Wood, who were appalled at the lack of overall military planning, wanted to establish an extensive military system to meet whatever contingency might arise. In 1914, the idea was given added impetus at the annual meeting of the National Civic Federation, where it was unanimously resolved that a "Council of Defense" be formed, with the president as its head and consisting of the secretaries of war and navy and the chairmen of the committees of the House and Senate on war and navy.[4] The function of the

2. Samuel Gompers, *Seventy Years of Life and Labor* (New York: E. P. Dutton and Company, 1925), 2: 350-51; Clarkson, *Industrial America*, pp. 12-13.
3. Arthur S. Link, *Wilson, Confusions and Crisis, 1915-1916* (Princeton: Princeton University Press, 1964), 4: 338-39.
4. Ralph Easley to Joseph P. Tumulty, December 6, 1914, NCF MSS.

Council was to report to Congress on legislation it considered necessary for national defense. Present at the meeting and voting for the resolution was Samuel Gompers. Shortly afterwards, Gompers claimed that he participated in the preparation of the resolution, and in quoting from the document he used the term "Council of National Defense."[5] Thus, fully six months before Woodrow Wilson had contemplated strengthening the nation's defense system, Gompers was already an advocate of measures that would further safeguard our national security.[6]

The proposal by the NCF did not envision fully the need to regulate industrial production to meet military requirements or to establish a civilian body with control over military supplies. Nevertheless, it did incorporate the concept of creating an agency with overall responsibility for the modernization of the nation's armed forces. However, if a relationship did exist between the Senate's designation of the agency as the Council of National Defense and the action of the NCF and Gompers, no evidence has yet been found to support it.

On October 11, 1916, Wilson named the seven members of the Advisory Commission. The one surprise was his choice of Samuel Gompers as one of the seven. Gompers readily accepted the appointment because he saw the "imperative need to have a spokesman for labor in the inner war council."[7] His conception of the CND as a "war council" was not accidental. He was soon to be speaking in terms of the "crisis which . . . was sure to come."[8] Besides, Wilson, in his opening address before the Advisory Commission, told the members that their function was to unite the country in peace as well as in war.[9]

5. Gompers to J. M. Wainwright, December 14, 1914, Gompers MSS.
6. While favoring the development of a Council of National Defense, Gompers also supported President Wilson in his opposition to the Gardner Resolution in Congress, strongly supported by advocates of military expansion, which sought to investigate the state of the nation's defense apparatus for the obvious purpose of strengthening it. "Its effect," said Gompers, "will be to agitate for war." The AFL leader feared that the military would attempt to capitalize on the war for the purpose of gaining from Congress increased expenditures for military purposes. However, he did not regard the creation of a Council of National Defense under the leadership of President Wilson as having the same effect. See *The Labor Herald* (December 25, 1914); Ralph Easley to Tumulty, December 6, 1914, NCF MSS.
7. Gompers, *Seventy Years*, 2: 351-52.
8. *Ibid.*, p. 146.
9. Ray Stannard Baker, *Woodrow Wilson: Life and Letters* (Garden City, N. Y.:

Gompers interpreted his appointment to the Advisory Commission as the first step in the granting to labor of a real voice in the inner circles of government. As a result, he was overly anxious to be of service. His anxiety was openly communicated to the secretary of war. He was so concerned lest he miss a single meeting or that the Administration form the opinion he was not willing to participate actively in carrying out his duties that he was constantly reiterating his good intentions and making sure that a meeting would not be called when he was unable to attend.[10] Gompers was true to his word. He threw himself wholeheartedly into the work of the Advisory Commission, laying aside all his other work and obligations in the interest of patriotism.[11]

Each member of the Advisory Commission was entitled to appoint a committee to aid him in carrying out his work. The formation of the Committee on Labor, with Gompers as chairman, was widely heralded as constituting "recognition of labor."[12] Its function was to recommend ways and means on how best to meet the needs of workers with the express purpose of eliminating industrial unrest. However, events were to prove that this committee had no effective powers and the work assigned to it was of relatively minor consequence.

Gompers's appointments to the Committee on Labor were representative of broad sections of labor and management. Included were some of the leading tycoons of the business community —August Belmont, John D. Rockefeller, Jr., Cornelius Vanderbilt, and Daniel Guggenheim—as well as a member of the National Association of Manufacturers, one of the most uncompromising and bitter enemies of the Federation. Through this committee both Wilson and Gompers hoped to secure the cooperation of labor and capital.[13] In the process, Gompers hoped for something more. He had slowly come to the conclusion that employer hostility to labor was not based on sound economic principles, but arose from an irrational fear that labor unions sought radically to alter the relations between manage-

Doubleday, Doran and Company, 1937), 6:308-9.
10. Gompers to Newton D. Baker, November 9, 1916, Gompers MSS.
11. Gompers to Clifford Pinchot, February 26, 1917, Gompers MSS.
12. Alexander Trachtenberg, ed., *The American Labor Year Book, 1917-18* (New York City: The Rand School of Social Science, 1919), p. 13.
13. Baker, *Woodrow Wilson: Life and Letters,* 7: 69.

ment and worker to the detriment of the former. If Gompers could convince the businessman that organized labor could be a major asset in helping to increase productivity, and thereby profits, he would achieve for the workingman by peaceful means standards that other labor movements could not gain through strikes. What was needed was for industry to become better acquainted with labor leaders, recognize their true worth and, as a result, possibly alter its misconceptions.[14] The Committee on Labor, to Gompers, thus had a dual objective: to help the country's war effort, and to bring about a *rapprochement* between capital and labor. He was to accomplish the former, but fail miserably in the latter.

The Advisory Commission, by its very nature, was to become the actual executive branch of the Council. Although its legal function was simply to advise, its advice was often accepted by the Council and acted upon. So powerful did the Commission become that the secretary of the Commission and Council, Grosvenor B. Clarkson, proudly quotes in his book from a report by Representative William J. Graham on what he called a "startling disclosure" of the "secret government of the United States."

> An examination of these minutes discloses the fact that a commission of seven men chosen by the President seems to have devised the entire system of purchasing war supplies, planned a press censorship, designed a system of food control and selected Herbert Hoover as its director , . . . and in a word designed practically every war measure which the Congress subsequently enacted, and did all this behind closed doors, weeks and even months before the Congress of the United States declared war against Germany.[15]

It was quite an achievement for a Commission of which Gompers was a member. However, within the Commission, Gompers was never given the share of duties, responsibilities, and power accorded other members of the body.

United States entrance into the conflict presented the Federation with two main problems: the extent to which it was willing to go to

14. Gompers, *Seventy Years,* 2: 366.
15. Clarkson, *Industrial America,* pp. 24-25.

enforce its demand for coequal representation on all industrial bodies connected with the war, and the degree of militancy it was willing to exert to improve working conditions at the bargaining table. The former was considered as indispensable if the AFL was to support its view that a new era had opened for labor. The latter raised all sorts of questions relating to wages and hours, strikes, the open and closed shop, and the Federation's attitude toward government intervention in the collective bargaining process. On all these issues the Federation took no firm position, fluctuating from one side to the other in relation to the degree of pressure brought on it by the government and the workers. However, it was to be mainly guided by the patriotic wartime demand for increasing productivity, with workers' needs subordinated to this primary objective. The union membership was of a different frame of mind and showed its displeasure by engaging in an unprecedented number of strikes, so that labor unrest became the major internal problem facing the nation.

Shortly after Congress declared war against Germany, Gompers issued a statement detailing the attitude of organized labor in reference to conditions of labor during wartime. It was released by the executive committee of the Committee on Labor and approved by the CND. Its significance lay in its outright advocacy of the prewar "status quo," and in its formulation of the general rule that during the war "neither employers nor employees shall endeavor to take advantage of the country's necessities to change existing standards." It further stated that if a situation arose that required change, it could "be made only after such proposed changes have been investigated and approved by the Council of National Defense."[16]

Labor's response to the statement left no doubt that the workers and local union leaders would accept no policy that condemned them to prewar standards, and accorded them no opportunity to improve their working conditions. Gompers's policy was interpreted as the result of a private agreement between the government, employers, and the president of the AFL, which guaranteed that organized labor would "remain quiet and raise no disturbance during the war."[17] It

16. The most important industrial documents of which the AFL was a signatory are reproduced in AFL, *Proceedings* (1917), pp. 82-88.
17. *The Blacksmiths' Journal* 19 (May 1917): 13-14.

was also seen as an assurance that organized labor would faithfully adhere to a no-strike policy for the duration of the conflict.

The uproar on the part of the rank and file of labor forced the Council to reinterpret its position and led Gompers to issue an emphatic denial. The government, conscious of the difficulties of the English and French with labor, vociferously denied that it had intended to use the emergency as a weapon to break down standards already achieved by labor or to deny labor the right to maintain conditions relative to the cost of living, but it did reaffirm its intention to see that the war was not used by employers or employees to gain ground that they were not able to achieve in peacetime.[18] Thus, the government tried to postpone industrial conflict until after the war.

Gompers, forced on the defensive, sought to assure his membership that he was opposed to any programs that would hinder their efforts to better their working conditions. Statements to the effect that he had agreed to a "no-strike policy" he dismissed as newspaper propaganda to discredit him.[19] Gompers denied that he had "made any promise to any one in any form that 'there shall be no strikes of any kind during the war.' "[20] Despite these denials, Gompers's prestige was injured. His supporters sought to restore his tarnished image by claiming that Gompers had actually outwitted anti-labor elements in that the Council's statement upheld labor safeguards by requiring that any law that tended to annul them had to be agreed to first by the Council.[21] Needless to say, the majority of organized labor was of a different opinion.

Whatever the merits of the controversy over what Gompers had agreed to, one fact is incontestable: he was not willing to use labor's newly won economic power during the war to gain for the working-

---

18. Newton D. Baker to Meyer London, May 8, 1917, cited by *Advance* (May 25, 1917).
19. Speech at organization of the American Alliance for Labor and Democracy, September 7, 1917, in Gompers, *American Labor and the War*, 112-13. *The New Republic* (April 14, 1917), pp. 312-13, and *The Tailor* (June 19, 1917), both agreed with Gompers.
20. Gompers to Daniel J. Tobin, April 17, 1917, Gompers MSS. See also *Machinists' Monthly Journal* 29 (May 1917): 460-61; *The Labor Herald* (April 6, 1917); Buton J. Hendrick, "The Leadership of Samuel Gompers," *The World's Work,* 35 (February 1918): 381-87.
21. *The Labor Herald* (May 4, 1917).

men and the trade unions what they had not been able to achieve before the war. He was willing to submerge all differences between labor and management,[22] and to struggle only to maintain the workingmen's standard of living, not to advance it.[23] As a result, during the early stages of the war, wages did not always keep pace with the soaring cost of living. It was only after worker dissatisfaction took the form of work stoppages or other acts that had the effect of decreasing productivity that working conditions began to improve and government heads became more attentive to the needs of wage earners. Thus, improvements in labor conditions during wartime resulted from the initiative of the rank and file and local labor leaders rather than from original pressures brought to bear by the AFL hierarchy on the Wilson Administration.

Gompers's overall plan for adjusting differences between labor and management was submitted to the Advisory Council on April 23. It suggested the creation of a National Board of Labor Adjustment, which was to consist of nine members: 2 representing labor, 2 representing industry, 3 representing the public, 1 woman, and 1 member of the United States Civil Service Commission. The Board's function, after conferring with representatives of employers and employees, was to establish minimum working standards in industries working on government contracts and to render a final decision on grievances that could not be settled on the plant level.[24]

Such a proposal was more than unusual, coming from the president of the AFL since its effect would be to strip labor of any final voice in the determination of working conditions. The ultimate decision in determining minimal standards or in settling grievances was

22. *New York Times,* May 1, 1917, p. 2.
23. At a conference at the Department of Labor, Secretary Wilson stated that neither employer nor employee should be able to "take advantage of the present abnormal conditions to establish new standards." He included the standard of living among these standards. Grant Hamilton, legislative committeeman of the AFL, agreed. See *Seamen's Journal* (May 16, 1917). Secretary of War Baker describes his understanding with Gompers as based on the agreement that the standard of living of the American worker would be maintained, in exchange for which labor agreed not to use the emergency to attempt to gain its prewar demands. See Newton D. Baker to John P. Frey, December 6, 1926, Frey MSS.
24. Franklin H. Martin, *Digest of the Proceedings of the Council of National Defense During the War* (Washington, D.C.: United States Government Printing Office, 1934), pp. 101-2.

to rest on the members representing the public and Civil Service Commission. Appointment power was to lie with the Council of National Defense and a real fear existed among those in accord with the objectives of organized labor that its public appointees might be of the "soldier type" and not too sympathetic with labor's aim. The establishment of the War Labor Board, as will be noted, contained greater structural safeguards for labor than Gompers's own proposal.

Gompers's agreement to a "status quo" arrangement is difficult to understand in light of the fact that organized labor now occupied a strategic bargaining position and, as a veteran negotiator, Gompers must have realized that for labor to grant a concession of such magnitude, it should be able to command equal reciprocity, especially from its principal antagonists.[25] Yet, at the time of the Council's announcement, Gompers granted business and the government most of what it asked without receiving equal compensatory assurances in return.

The proposal by the Committee on Labor of the Advisory Commission was given concrete form on June 19, 1917, when, for the first time in history, a labor union was to enter an agreement with the United States government. A memorandum was signed between Gompers and Secretary of War Baker providing that in cantonment construction the prevailing union scale of wages and hours was to apply. In exchange for this concession, Gompers orally agreed to the open shop. Difficulty arose when it became apparent that it was possible to read into the agreement that the government favored the closed shop. Louis B. Wehle, assistant to Secretary Baker, asked Gompers to confirm in writing his oral agreement. Gompers immediately wired that the Memorandum "had reference to union hours and wages; the question of union shop was not included."[26]

Under the memorandum, a Labor Adjustment Board was established for the express purpose of adjusting labor disputes arising

25. Maintenance of the "status quo" was the principal demand of the employers throughout the war. They never wavered from this position. See Alexander M. Bing, *War Time Strikes and Their Adjustment* (New York: E. P. Dutton & Company, 1921), p. 153; Martin, *Digest of Proceedings,* pp. 259-60.

26. Gompers to Louis Wehle, June 22, 1917, Gompers MSS. In his Autobiography and in AFL, *Proceedings* (1917), no mention is made of Gompers's wire or his acceptance of the open shop. Only the original agreement was included in both.

under the agreement. The Board was to consist of three persons; one representing the army, one the public, and one labor. Eventually, additional memorandums were signed extending this agreement to all construction work carried on by the War Department, the Navy Department, and the Emergency Fleet Corporation.

As noted previously, the remarkable feature of Gompers's signing was that he agreed to the memorandum without the express authorization of the Executive Council or Convention, and in direct violation of the AFL constitution, which granted absolute autonomy to the national and international unions making up the Federation. Clearly, Gompers's assent was not binding on the membership. Furthermore, the national unions had traditionally followed a policy of refusing to allow their members to work alongside nonunion workers. As a result, Secretary of War Baker had seriously doubted that Gompers would ever agree to "concede the open shop for any consideration."[27] However, Gompers's agreement did have the intended effect. Many union leaders, openly loath to repudiate their chief, assented to the terms of the Gompers-Baker Memorandum. There were some notable exceptions, William Hutcheson of the Carpenters, for one, who refused to abandon the closed shop and waged a struggle in its behalf.

By the fall of 1917, it had become apparent that the labor adjustment boards had not served the function of stabilizing industrial relations. A multiplicity of problems were involved in labor unrest and the opinion had slowly formed that only a centralized agency under government control could standardize working conditions and put an end to the strikes and lockouts that were plaguing the economy. It was further proposed that a national labor policy be created under an agency that would be in close touch with those responsible for production. Gompers had hoped that this task would be given to the Advisory Commission, particularly his Committee on Labor. This would have assured labor representation in the all-important matter of drawing up a blueprint to govern employer-employee relations for the duration of the war. Instead, the president decided to all but incorporate the Committee on Labor into the War Labor Administration,

27. Louis B. Wehle, *Hidden Threads of History* (New York: Macmillan Company, 1953), p. 20.

which was to reside in the Department of Labor and be under the control of the secretary of labor, William B. Wilson.

As War Labor Administrator, Secretary Wilson proceeded to form an Advisory Council, composed of representatives of labor and management, to advise him on the administration of labor matters. Its suggestion led to the formation of the War Labor Conference Board, which had the task of formulating a comprehensive set of rules to guide employer-employee relations.

The Board consisted of five members chosen by the AFL and five by the employer's association, the National Industrial Conference Board. Each group selected a chairman, who was to serve on alternate days. The labor representatives selected Frank P. Walsh, while the employers named former President William Howard Taft. On April 8, President Wilson appointed the members to act as a National War Labor Board.

Among the principles that guided the Board was the right of workers to organize and bargain collectively through representatives of their own choosing; protection of workers against discharge for union membership; preservation of the union shop and union conditions where they already existed; and, where the union shop did not exist and the employer met only with employees of his own establishment, the continuance of such a procedure would not be deemed a grievance. Workers were forbidden to use coercive measures of any kind to induce prospective members to join their union, or to pressure employers to deal with their organization. Strikes and lockouts were also forbidden, and the right of all workers to a living wage was accepted. Although the Board had no statutory authority, its vast powers lay in the war emergency—the pressure of public opinion, and the emergency powers of the president to ensure an uninterrupted flow of production.

Organized labor accepted the principles of the Board much more readily than the employers. Credit for employer acquiescence belongs mainly to ex-President Taft, who had to read the "riot act" to his followers to get them to go along.[28] Employer reluctance was due to a desire to maintain the *status quo* on the open shop, a shop in which

28. Henry F. Pringle, *The Life and Times of William Howard Taft* (New York: Farrar & Rinehart, Inc., 1939), 2:917.

employers could refuse to employ union men and discharge them if they joined the union. Taft wrote that the employers did not wish to make this view "prominent and so they 'pussyfooted' about it and they got left."[29]

In contrast, Gompers wrote of the Board as a "wonderful achievement."[30] He was not alone in this view. Even some of the more militant unions regarded the Board as setting a new standard in the history of industrial development.[31] The Sailors' Union went so far as to see itself freed from the day-to-day struggle for shorter hours and higher wages, since it saw the joint board created by the government as taking care of these problems.[32] Following this logic, the union felt its main area of concentration should be on developing fundamental economic changes rather than on everyday working conditions.[33] What was more ominous for the labor movement, the union accepted employer willingness to go along with the Board as representing either a basic change of policy, or, if not, as indicating the ability of the government to impose its view on the employers. This may have been true in the short run, but, as events were to prove, the assumptions were to break down completely once the war was over.

The recognition by employers of labor's right to organize in trade unions and to bargain collectively was of transcending importance to the AFL leaders. They perceived this as a highly significant step toward bringing about industrial peace after the war.[34] Very little thought was given to the possibility that the amity between labor and capital generated by the war would founder on the reef of implacable employer hostility once the pressing need for such cooperation disappeared. If this contingency should arise, the Federation felt certain that the workings of the Board, its legal procedures and decisions, would constitute such a body of legal and procedural precedence as to shape future practice.

That employers were determined to maintain the open shop soon

29. *Ibid.*, 2: 919.
30. Gompers to Executive Council, March 30, 1918, Gompers MSS.
31. *Seamen's Journal* (April 17, 1918).
32. *Ibid.*
33. *Ibid.*
34. *Machinists' Monthly Journal* 30 (May 1918), pp. 481-82.

became evident in the dispute between the Commercial Telegraphers' Union and the Western Union Telegraph Company. The dispute centered around the refusal of Western Union to reinstate workers discharged for union activity. After considering the issues involved, the War Labor Board granted the employees the right to join a union and ordered the reinstatement of all discharged workers. It also directed that the company was not obligated to deal with the union or recognize it. Although the Supreme Court had upheld the validity of the "yellow-dog" contract,[35] it was agreed that its implementation would be suspended for the duration of the war. The continued refusal of Western Union to accept the Board's ruling eventually led President Wilson to seek authorization from Congress to take over the telegraph and telephone lines in order to force compliance.[36]

While the union readily agreed to the Board's decision, the terms of agreement did not provide it with any opportunity to build a stable organizational base upon which it could either expand its membership among Western Union workers or instill in them a fighting trade-union spirit so as to be able to withstand the open hostility of management, which was certain to accelerate once the wartime restrictions were over. The failure of the Commercial Telegraphers' Union to use economic pressure to compel management to recognize the union and to secure the closed shop, particularly at a period when the shortage of labor gave it a tactical advantage, was bound to weaken the solidarity of the workers, since the company, at the end of the war, could again resort to the "yellow-dog" contract and bring unbearable pressure to bear upon those workers who had displayed any degree of loyalty to the union.

Although labor was enamored with the principles of the War Labor Board, it was bound to be weakened by being tied to it. By relinquishing its right to strike and its demand for the closed shop, organized labor surrendered the major weapons it possessed. Thus, for its sheer existence and future prosperity, it placed its main reliance on government support. This operated to tie the Federation even more closely to the foreign policies enunciated by Woodrow Wilson.

35. *Hitchman Coal & Coke Co.* v. *Mitchell,* 245 U.S. 229, 38 Sup. Ct. 65.
36. Gompers to Newton D. Baker, January 23, 1918, Gompers MSS; Baker, *Woodrow Wilson: Life and Letters,* 8: 205-7.

In order to provide for "central authority and decisive information" for the war-industry needs of the nation, the Council of National Defense on July 8, 1917, formed the War Industries Board. Its function was to manipulate the entire industrial resources of the country for the purpose of coordinating military needs with industrial output. Since labor was crucial to production, Hugh Frayne, an AFL organizer, was chosen as labor commissioner.

Grosvenor Clarkson, quite candidly and a bit startlingly, sets forth the main purpose behind Frayne's appointment. His task, writes the former secretary to the Advisory Commission and Council, "was not . . . to represent labor, but to manage it."[37] Like Gompers, Frayne did his work so well as to earn the adulation of many of the nation's leaders for giving "first consideration to the demands of country as against those of special interest."[38] It was an era when labor "statesmanship" was in full flower.

Among Frayne's many duties, supplying and allocating skilled labor seems to have been of major importance. The War Department notified all its units that Frayne had proved to be of great help in obtaining skilled workers, and that they should not hesitate to use his assistance.[39] Clarkson estimates that through his assistance over 125,000 workers were recruited for war work, mostly for special emergencies.[40]

In obtaining skilled labor, the Government made full use of the agencies established by the AFL unions to marshall the needed manpower. The United States Employment Service proved unequal to the task, and the trade-union centers became virtual hiring halls, recruiting and dispensing manpower according to government specifications.[41] When the need arose for motor mechanics to go to France, it was the craft unions that assisted in filling the quota.[42] In

---

37. Clarkson, *Industrial America*, p. 276.
38. *Ibid.*, pp. 92, 278; Margaret L. Coit, *Mr. Baruch* (Boston: Houghton Mifflin Company, 1957), p. 166.
39. Memorandum from Colonel H. E. Pierce to The Chief Signal Officer of the War Department, undated, W. I. B. Files, 8-A1, National Archives.
40. Clarkson, *Industrial America*, p. 278.
41. *The Carpenter* 38 (February 1918): 13-14; *Machinists' Monthly Journal* 30 (February 1918): 163.
42. *Ibid.*

actual operation, the AFL became an indispensable adjunct of the Employment Service.

Recruitment of skilled labor was not the only industrial service offered by the Federation to the government and industry. The Federation became a partner with management in helping to stimulate productivity. Various efficiency plans emanated from the union leaders. However, they had to step carefully due to traditional worker hostility to such plans. The presidents of the Boilermakers and Machinists Unions promoted such a plan on the Baltimore & Ohio Railroad but demurred from calling it a "union efficiency" plan because they feared opposition from the workers.[43] Instead, it was referred to as "union-management cooperation."

Meanwhile, Gompers worked diligently to see that his members patriotically endeavored to increase production. If information came to him that union members in a particular plant were not exerting themselves fully in behalf of the war effort, he would so notify the government and ask for an investigation.[44] In effect, he was asking the Department of Labor to investigate his own membership to their possible detriment. Of course, Gompers and the national union leadership did not care to take the matter up themselves for fear of incurring the wrath of the membership.[45]

Gompers also endeavored to curtail the efforts of local trade unions that sought to gain raises for their membership well beyond increases in the cost of living. He was not averse to informing government officials that, in his opinion, such raises were unjustified. Gompers supported his position on very righteous and practical grounds. "But how can we union leaders," he appealed to Wehle, ". . . hold our moral claim on the American people if we help put the screws on them now by exploiting their great need in time of war?"[46] However, the pursuit of such a policy by the AFL leadership was to bring an indignant response from its constituency.

---

43. Wehle, *Hidden Threads,* pp. 65-66.
44. Gompers to William B. Wilson, August 21, 1917, Gompers MSS.
45. *Ibid.*
46. Wehle, *Hidden Threads,* p. 25.

7

The Struggle for Labor's Rights

Fundamental to Gompers's support of Wilson's foreign policies was rank-and-file acceptance of his domestic program. During the four years of the European War, Gompers's approach to industrial problems was largely molded by events occurring overseas. His grand design for labor, which hinged on the hope that the working class would sacrifice immediate gain for the promise of a future of plenty, was to suffer its severest test in 1917 as millions of workers voiced their uneasiness over an economic policy based on passivity and lack of militancy.

Recognizing the disinclination of his membership to sacrifice any of their gains or to accept any agreement based on prewar conditions, Gompers sought to build an attractive ideological structure to justify the Federation's position. It was a case of trying to "sell" the war to an already suspicious and hard-to-convince workingman. The AFL thus took the position that if the war was being fought for democractic principles, as Wilson stated, then these same principles must be present at home. If labor was to be asked to sacrifice, then surely it could ask for no less than equality of representation with all other interests on all government boards and agencies concerned with the prosecution of the war.

Equality of representation was to be given its first real test in the appointment of Gompers to the Advisory Commission of the CND, and in the creation of the Committee on Labor, of which he was to be chairman. But it soon became apparent that labor representation was strictly limited to those committees dealing with labor disputes, and that labor was pointedly excluded from those agencies and committees which controlled the distribution of government contracts.[1] The Committees on Supplies, Transportation and Communication, and their vast subcommittees covering almost every commodity for which the government had a need, were without labor representation and made up exclusively of bankers, merchants, and industrialists.[2] Contracts were distributed with little thought given to the needs of the workers, but with sole regard to economy and speed of production. As a result, nonunion firms were rewarded with the bulk of government contracts.

The one production committee upon which organized labor was granted representation was formed only through the willingness of the trade union involved to demand and fight for this right. Seeking to increase productivity and reduce labor turnover, the Coal Production Committee proposed to restrict a miner's ability to move from job to job. President White of the United Mine Workers denounced the act and declared that the union would refuse to cooperate with a Committee that did not have on it a single labor representative. The result was that on June 15, 1917, seven labor men were added to the thirteen employer and government officials already on the Committee. It was labor's first big victory for equal representation, and it

1. Alexander Trachtenberg, ed., *The American Labor Year Book, 1917-1918* (New York: The Rand School of Social Science, 1919) pp. 10, 15; Lewis L. Lorwin, *The American Federation of Labor* (Washington, D.C.: Brookings Institution, 1933), pp. 158-59. The demand of organized labor for "democratic management" of the industrial sector was not treated seriously by the CND but regarded as mere public relations. Perhaps the attitude of many industrialists and government officials was best expressed by the director of the CND, W. S. Gifford, who looked upon Gompers's appointment to the Advisory Commission in itself as granting to labor full and total recognition and representation. See *Coast Seamen's Journal* (March 28, 1917).
2. *The New Republic* (July 7, 1917), p. 264.

was brought about only through the strength and pugnacity of the UMW.[3]

If labor did not achieve equal representation on all boards and agencies formed by the national government, it fared no better on the local level. In fact, the few examples available indicate that its plight was much worse in the local communities. In July 1918, over a year after American participation in the war, the Wood, Wire and Metal Lathers' International Union complained that in the entire County of Lee, Illinois, not a single labor representative sat on any committee, no matter how small.[4] The Peoria Building Trades Council suffered a similar experience. Businessmen of the city of Peoria, no matter how many times they were requested to do so, had refused to add a representative of labor to any of the war committees. Exasperated and embittered, the labor unions were considering calling a mass meeting of all labor in Peoria and protesting to the government in Washington.[5] There is no reason to believe these were isolated instances.

The failure of labor to achieve equal representation struck a crippling blow at Gompers's entire program. He had based his foreign and domestic policies on the premise that the democratic objectives of the Wilson Administration guaranteed to the workingman not only a voice in the determination of his own working conditions, but on all questions concerned with wartime production. Yet, Gompers took such a position without receiving "definite assurances" from the president.[6] The most that Wilson would grant was to say that he thought it "fair and wise" that representatives of labor be on all boards dealing with industrial questions.[7] Thus Gompers had built his

3. Trachtenberg, *American Labor Year Book, 1917-18,* p. 12. See also Lorwin, *American Federation of Labor,* pp. 156-57.
4. John Madick to American Federation of Labor, July 25, 1918, Department of Labor Files, 20/673, National Archives.
5. Peoria Building Trades Council to William B. Wilson, June 20, 1918, Department of Labor Files, 20/629, National Archives.
6. Woodrow Wilson to Tumulty, September 17, 1917, Wilson MSS.
7. *Ibid.* See also Bernard I. Bell to Tumulty, September 17, 1917, Wilson MSS.

foundation on the vagaries of hope rather than on a concrete *quid pro quo* achieved through negotiation with the government.

Under growing pressure from the membership, the AFL began to insist that the Council of National Defense grant labor representation "coequal with all other interests, upon all agencies, boards, committees and commissions entrusted with war work."[8] This was followed up by a visit with President Wilson. The president of the Illinois Federation of Labor and the chief officers of the Chicago Federation of Labor, accompanied by Gompers, informed the president of the necessity of granting labor direct representation on all effective contract-handling committees of the CND like that already won by the United Mine Workers in the Coal Production Committee.[9]

Meanwhile, labor journalists were reporting that the refusal of the CND and the War and Navy Departments to recognize the right of trade unionists to serve on committees letting war contracts was leading to a summer of industrial demands and probably numerous large strikes.[10] It was a sore that was to fester openly during the entire war period.

It was to Gompers's credit that throughout the war he never hesitated to assert labor's right to representation on all war agencies, even the most obscure ones.[11] His failure lay not so much in his persistence in demanding labor's rights, but rather in his unwillingness to go beyond the state of articulation—or in modern terminology, *jawboning*—and attempt to achieve his aims through some concrete act. Toward the end of 1917, it had become all too apparent that Gompers was so tied to Wilson's war program, and so committed to his belief that labor could secure its future only through unquestioned

8. Gompers and Frank Morrison to Council of National Defense, June 27, 1917, Gompers MSS. The letter also went to great lengths to assure the Council that labor was "in wholehearted accord with the declarations of President Wilson as to the causes for which the republic of the United States has entered the war. . . ." Gompers seemed to find it necessary to balance his dissent on a particular issue with professions of loyalty to the country.

9. *Coast Seamen's Journal* (August 29, 1917).

10. *Ibid.* (July 11, 1917).

11. Gompers to Benedict Crowell, April 18, 1918, Gompers MSS. Gompers wrote the War Department asking for representation on the Research Information Committee, which was concerned with research into mathematical, physical, and biological sciences. He based his claim on the obvious knowledge that the human factor was present in all work and could not be overlooked.

support of and cooperation with the government, that he sought to justify labor's failure to gain equal representation on government boards by either directly or indirectly denying that failure. Thus, at the 1917 AFL convention, the report of the Executive Council gave added emphasis to labor representatives serving on government boards while neglecting to mention that labor had gained very little in this area.[12] By February 1918, Gompers was declaring with finality that this principle for which labor had long contended had been recognized in most departments of the government.[13] A few months later, in a speech before the National Lecturers' Association, Gompers proclaimed that labor had achieved a degree of representation greater "than at any time in the history of our country, or perhaps the whole world."[14] However, contrary to Gompers's assertion, organized labor was never able to realize its demand for equal representation on all government boards and agencies dealing with industrial matters.

Wilson's desire to treat labor fairly was not automatically transferred to a host of lesser government officials who were in charge of handling labor problems and of issuing government contracts. Bureaucratic ideas and practices, conditioned by years of anti-union hostility and lack of concern about the human factor in production, caused government contracts to be granted in ever-increasing numbers to nonunion firms. This was not only undermining union strength, but it also served to depress wage standards. The situation became particularly acute in Philadelphia. The Quartermaster's Department in the city, for reasons known only to itself, placed most of the contracts in that city with unorganized firms where the cheapest labor was used and where the physical plant was ill equipped to do the work.[15] This resulted in most of the work's being subcontracted to small tenement operations where working conditions were at their worst. The situation was developing into a major threat to the garment unions.

12. AFL, *Proceedings* (1917), p. 81.
13. Speech on Washington's Birthday, February 22, 1918, in Samuel Gompers, *American Labor and the War* (New York: George H. Doran Company, 1919), pp. 180-81.
14. Gompers, *American Labor and the War*, p. 192.
15. *The New Republic* (July 7, 1917), pp. 263-65.

At first, Gompers maintained an air of indifference to complaints from the garment workers. He explained to the United Garment Workers that since government contracts were controlled by law, the lowest bidder was usually successful, and since it was impractical to attempt to change the law at this time, the best possible course for the union to follow was to be patient and wait because so many government conracts were in the offing that some were bound to be let to union shops.[16] In effect, Gompers took a hands-off position and did not deem it necessary to use his office to seek redress of the union's grievance.

However, by July, as complaints multiplied, Gompers indicated that he was willing to take some action. The hat workers found that nonunion manufacturers, exploiting their underpaid workers, were accepting lower bids and getting government contracts. Union firms, unable to compete because of union wage scales, were resorting to the practice of subcontracting their work to nonunion shops in order to be able to bid low enough to get government work.[17] Moreover, the union had remained relatively quiet because it was under the impression that the Federation had obtained an agreement with the government that contracts would go only to those firms using the union label.[18] Gompers, slowly being forced on the defensive, no longer counseled a policy of waiting, but wrote to the War Department asking for action.[19] His activity took the form of a request for fairness to the Secretary of War, and it is doubtful if he pursued the matter much further.

As a general rule, top officials of the Wilson Administration, except for Postmaster General Burleson, were responsive to labor's needs and acted accordingly. Problems most often occurred in the lower layers of the bureaucracy or on some of the newly created boards that were largely staffed with businessmen who shared an anti-union bias. A prime example was the United States Shipping Board, which was under the chairmanship of a confirmed opponent of trade unionism, Edward N. Hurley. Its policies, at times, seemed designed to provoke the craft unions.

16. Gompers to G. A. Ott, May 7, 1917, Gompers MSS.
17. M. Zaritsky to Gompers, July 7, 1917, Gompers MSS.
18. *Ibid.*
19. Gompers to Newton D. Baker, July 18, 1917, Gompers MSS.

The Building Trades Department of the AFL had protested to the Shipping Board the letting of a contract for the construction of houses to a contractor who was hostile to organized labor. Upon assurances from the Board that this would not happen again, the Department withdrew its protest.[20] Almost immediately, the Board violated its agreement by letting a contract to a firm equally antagonistic to labor. Gompers charged that the board was taking advantage of the war to strengthen the opponents of trade unionism.[21] But Gompers's charge lacked the force to compel compliance. It was another appeal to patriotism and sought to instruct the Board on how best to win the war and accelerate construction work by cooperating with labor instead of fighting it.

Adding to the discomfiture of the Federation leadership was the appearance in September 1917 of documented charges by Amos Pinchot that some of the business representatives of the CND were using their positions to extract exorbitant profits from the war.[22] This was not the only case of using the crisis for personal gain. The unconscionable gouging for wartime profits was admitted by the industrialists themselves. Bernard Baruch had been vexed at the attitude of the copper magnates who, as Senator Bennett Champ Clark charged, "held a gun to Uncle Sam" in order to exact enormous profits.[23] *The Wall Street Journal* castigated the steel industry for charging prices that were "utterly indefensible."[24] Supporting this statement was the admission of the president of the McKinney Steel Company that he was "making more money out of this war than the average human being ought to."[25]

Publicity given to some of the above statements was undermining Gompers's entire approach to the war, which was based on the principle of equality of sacrifice. The American workingman had largely

20. Gompers to Edward N. Hurley, May 24, 1917, Gompers MSS.
21. *Ibid.*
22. Amos Pinchot to Conference Committees of Senate and House of Representatives, September 18, 1917, cited by *Machinists' Monthly Journal* 29 (October 1917): 860-62.
23. Margaret L. Coit, *Mr. Baruch* (Boston: Houghton Mifflin Company, 1957), p. 169.
24. Quoted by *Coast Seamen's Journal* (October 3, 1917).
25. Grosvenor B. Clarkson, *Industrial America in the World War* (Boston and New York: Houghton Mifflin Company, 1924), pp. 318-19.

been of the opinion that wars were the product of evil men and rapacious economic forces that sought to profit from them. In order to secure support for Wilson's policies, Gompers assured his membership that the war was not in the interest of one class, but of all the American people, and that no group would profit at the expense of another. At the moment Congress declared war against Germany, the AFL was confidently predicting that Wall Street had "agreed that the day for unbridled war profits [was] gone," and that the Administration in Washington was determined to end wartime exploitation.[26] Furthermore, the Federation optimistically reported, the president was ready to use recently passed legislation empowering him to seize any plant that he believed was unduly profiting from the war.[27]

The Federation's claim that it would not use the emergency to advance its own interests was not idle boasting. In its strenuous effort to appear reasonable and patriotic, the Federation leaders actually went to the extent of failing to obtain better working conditions for their membership when their economic power would easily have enabled them to do so. This was admitted by the president of the Building Trades Department of the AFL, John H. Donlin, who in a moment of patriotic fervor confessed that he did not always get for his memberships what he "should" or what he was "able to compel."[28] Coupled with the disclosures of wartime profiteering, AFL economic policies were bound to spark increasing dissatisfaction among rank-and-file trade unionists.

Prior to the war, the AFL had stressed the closed shop as the primary demand to be made upon employers at the negotiating table. This was not arbitrarily arrived at, but rested on the fact that not only the union's strength, but its very existence would be determined by its ability to gain this point. Yet, during the initial period of the war, Gompers, in return for government acceptance of union wages and hours, yielded on labor's demand for a union shop. It was to be the greatest economic concession made by labor during the war. As

26. *Coast Seamen's Journal* (April 25, 1917).
27. *Ibid.*
28. John H. Donlin to Louis B. Wehle, September 4, 1917, cited by Louis B. Wehle, *Hidden Threads of History* (New York: Macmillan Company, 1953), pp. 36-37.

such, some of the leaders of the national and international unions refused to accept it, notably William L. Hutcheson of the Carpenters.[29]

The Carpenters, a conservative union, believed that the union had to wage a consistent struggle to maintain its rights.[30] Hutcheson viewed the union shop as the "foundation upon which all other conditions rested."[31] For this reason, he refused to enter into any agreement with the government that would place the union in a position of having acquiesced to the open shop.

Hutcheson's stubbornness placed a dagger at the heart of Gompers's *status quo* policy. His grandiose hopes of aligning labor with government and industry in a new postwar industrial order was in danger of being torpedoed due to management's unalterable hostility to the union shop, and with it an end to industrial peace, which the government so ardently desired. In seeking to resolve the situation, it was typical of Gompers to put all possible pressure upon the union to get it to change its position while completely absolving the government of its stand. Gompers sought refuge in legalistic arguments. He upheld the government's contention that it could not legally enter into such agreements. The government of the United States, emphasized Gompers, "representing all the people of the United States cannot enter into an agreement to employ exclusively members of any one organization."[32] Hutcheson was unmoved by Gompers's logic and was a constant thorn to Gompers and the government throughout the war. He eventually provoked Wilson to ask his now-famous question: "Will you cooperate or will you obstruct?"[33]

The importance of Hutcheson's position has generally been ignored by labor historians. The closed shop provided that all workers in an

29. In *Hidden Threads,* pp. 40-44, Wehle relates how, in concert with Gompers, he was able to obtain acceptance of the open shop from some of the national and international presidents.
30. *The Carpenter* 27 (March 1917): 4.
31. Maxwell C. Raddock, *Portrait of an American Labor Leader: William L. Hutcheson* (New York: American Institute of Social Science, Inc., 1955), p. 88.
32. Gompers to William L. Hutcheson, October 2, 1917, Gompers MSS; Gompers to William L. Hutcheson, October 16, 1917, Gompers MSS.
33. Woodrow Wilson to William L. Hutcheson, February 17, 1918, Ray Stannard Baker, *Woodrow Wilson: Life and Letters* (Garden City, N. Y.: Doubleday, Doran and Company, 1939), 7:550-51.

industrial unit would be members of the union and subject to its control and discipline. If a dispute arose with an employer, the union, in the event it wanted to take direct action, would be assured of solidarity among the workers. In the absence of a closed shop, the employers retained the ability to play off union members against nonunion workers, thereby blocking the union from taking any concerted measures, and demonstrating its ineffectiveness before the workers. The result inevitably led to the destruction of the union and the flowering of the open shop.

By obtaining agreement to union wages and hours as well as union recognition from the government, the AFL won important gains for the labor movement. But these achievements, by themselves, did not provide the kind of security or organizational structure necessary to ward off potential attacks from employers. A minimal degree of safety could have been accomplished only through the adoption of the closed or union shop. Gompers's position would have been sound had he been given a firm commitment of government support and business cooperation after the war. Lacking both, he was bound to fail. Postwar events were to prove how slender were the reeds Gompers built his policies on.

It was to be expected that the Federation would use its advantageous position during the war years to organize the overwhelming number of workers still outside its ranks. But Gompers was wedded to a policy of minimizing labor disturbances and so dampened any such efforts. He told John L. Lewis that he had arrived at an agreement with Woodrow Wilson to maintain the *status quo,* and this forbade any such activity as a union-organizing drive.[34] Following Gompers's lead, the Minnesota State Federation of Labor agreed to comply with a state law that prohibited union organizing during the war, and entered into an agreement with the Minnesota Employers' Association that if an employer before the war had refused to employ union labor, he would be permitted to continue to do so.[35]

34. Saul Alinsky, *John L. Lewis* (New York: G. P. Putnam's Sons, 1949), p. 28. Lewis regarded this as a major mistake and vowed he would never permit himself to become so obligated to an administration as to paralyze him from acting in the best interests of labor.

35. Alexander M. Bing, *War Time Strikes and Their Adjustment* (New York: E. P. Dutton and Company, 1921), pp. 164-65.

Leading steel producers made no secret of the fact that they had relied "for industrial peace . . . upon the assurances publicly given the Administration by the heads of the Federation that no attempts would be made to organize non-union works until after the war."[36] As a result, no major attempt was made during the war to organize the steel industry, despite organized labor's increased strength and the ability of the steel companies to pay higher wages because of increased profits.

In spite of Gompers's indifference to organizing the unorganized, union membership more than doubled during the war years. Most of the gains occurred in industries that were already highly organized rather than in those areas where nonunionism predominated.[37] Gains in union membership were due primarily to the increased demand for workers in trades that were engaged in war work, and to the action of the government, which had taken the role, both directly and indirectly, of a large employer.[38] Thus, the Boilermakers attributed their growth to the importance of shipbuilding at the time, and to the government's taking over the railroads and neutralizing employer hostility.[39] However, not all the unions viewed the government as a positive factor aiding organization. The Machinists felt that the war would retard their organization of workers employed on railroads in the Northeast.[40]

As a result of its *status quo* agreement with the government, coupled with its outmoded craft form of organization, the Federation failed to draw into its ranks millions of workers at a time when it was in a strategic position to do so. At the end of the war, it still represented only a small fraction of the entire working force.

When Gompers was first accused of pledging labor to a no-strike policy, he indignantly denied it. Yet, the Federation did pursue a policy that, in all but name, virtually sought to ban strikes. It created a

36. *New York Times*, September 24, 1917, p. 11.
37. Harry A. Millis and Royal E. Montgomery, *Organized Labor* (New York: McGraw-Hill Book Company, 1945), p. 133.
38. The government often urged management to allow union organization and not seek to repress it, since such activity acted as a safety valve and prevented more violent explosions. See William B. Wilson to James L. Davidson, June 9, 1917, Baker, *Woodrow Wilson: Life and Letters*, 7:111.
39. *The Boilermakers' Journal* 30 (April 1918): 336-37.
40. *Machinists' Monthly Journal* 29 (May 1917): 459.

structure composed of moral guidelines that made any work stoppage suspect on patriotic grounds. In a letter to all trade-union officers, Gompers set forth the rules governing strikes in wartime. "No strike ought to be inaugurated," he said, "that cannot be justified to the men facing momentary death. A strike during the war is not justified," Gompers continued, "unless principles are involved equally fundamental as those for which fellow citizens have offered their lives—their all."[41] Clearly, using such criteria, no strike could be readily justified. But even where a strike would have been justifiable because of employer intransigence, Gompers urged his men to be patient, sometimes beyond normal endurance, so as not to interrupt production.[42] By 1918, some of the more militant unions began to accept Gompers's criteria. The United Mine Workers and the Electrical Workers even went a step further. Viewing the government as an ally of labor and protector of its interests, they agreed to "lay aside for the time being, and if the experiment is successful for all time, its weapon of defense—the strike. . . ."[43]

If appeals to patriotism were not effective in preventing strikes, Gompers used the power of his office to produce the desired results. Often, this was done in utter disregard of the welfare of the workers. The winning of the war and the AFL's promise to the Wilson Administration to maintain industrial peace took precedence over local conditions where workers' grievances obviously called for a remedy that could be obtained only through some form of direct action. An excellent example was the labor situation in Puerto Rico.

Working conditions on the island were deplorable. "The attitude of the employers . . . toward their employees is that of the old Spanish bourbons toward their slaves," wrote Gompers to the office of the secretary of war.[44] Responding to an appeal from the Puerto Rican unions, Gompers beseeched the War Department to take steps to end

41. Gompers to All Trade Union Officers, April 8, 1918, Gompers MSS.
42. Speech at Convention of National Lecturers' Association, April 11, 1918, in Gompers, *American Labor and the War*, p. 194. Other union presidents endorsed Gompers's position. See statement by Charles H. Moyer, President of International Union of Mine, Mill and Smelter Workers in *Coast Seamen's Journal* (December 11, 1917).
43. *United Mine Workers' Journal* (June 20, 1918), p. 15.
44. Gompers to B. H. Getchell, February 28, 1918, Gompers MSS.

the unrelieved misery of the workers. Yet, little effort was made to alleviate their plight or deal with their complaints, with the result that the restiveness of the workers finally led to the calling of a strike. Communication between the Federation and the Puerto Rican labor locals provides a tawdry example of how Gompers's intimate relations with the government corroded his ability to act directly in behalf of his own membership, and led the AFL into a state of inactivity, if not indifference.

In December 1917, workers employed in Puerto Rican sugar mills and affiliated with the AFL applied to Gompers for the right to strike. Not having received permission by March, the local's leaders, in an exasperated tone, informed Gompers that they were tired of waiting for practical results from the arbitrator, "and even tired to the utmost awaiting your authority to declare ourselves in strike. . . ."[45] Furthermore, they requested information as to whether they would be entitled to strike benefits under the AFL Constitution if they refused to cross picket lines of other agricultural workers.[46] If refused strike authorization because of Gompers's "irresolution," the local declared, they would be forced either to become strikebreakers against the principles of the Federation or go on strike without the support of the AFL.[47]

Having received no reply to its communication of March 18, the local union notified Gompers on March 26 that more than 2,000 agricultural workers were now on strike, and that the Federation members were also induced to stop work in order not to become strikebreakers. Again it requested information on strike benefits.[48] Again, Gompers did not answer.

45. Higinio Lovan and J. Santos Rodriguez, to Gompers, March 18, 1918, Gompers MSS. For a discussion of strikes in Puerto Rico during 1917-1918, see Government of Puerto Rico, Bureau of Labor, *Special Bulletin of Bureau of Labor on Strikes in Puerto Rico During Fiscal Year 1917-1918.*
46. *Ibid.* Under Article XII of the Constitution of the AFL the Executive Council had the power to exact a levy on all affiliated unions for the purpose of assisting in a strike or lockout. Article XIII specifically stated that in no circumstances could moneys be disbursed from the defense fund to any Local Trade Union or Federal Labor Union without having been first authorized and approved by the president and executive council. This placed enormous power in Gompers's hands in his dealings with these small locals.
47. *Ibid.*
48. Higinio Lovan and J. Santos Rodriguez, to Gompers, March 26, 1918, Gompers MSS.

By April 9, the secretary of the Local, under pressure from the membership and reacting to the tension of a long strike, pleaded with Gompers to "at least do us the honor of a reply."[49] He bluntly informed Gompers that the union was losing ground and if the strike were lost, the blame would rest solely on the AFL. Should this happen, he wrote, it would mean an end of Federation membership in the area.[50]

The records do not indicate that Gompers ever did give the Puerto Rican local "the honor of a reply." Finally, five months after a reply had been requested, Gompers arrived at a decision and conveyed his answer. Curiously, he did not seek to respond directly to the local involved, but sought, instead, to communicate his decision to the AFL General Organizer from Puerto Rico, Santiago Iglesias, who was in Washington at the time. Part of the explanation may lie in the fact that all AFL organizers were appointed by the president and subject to his control. In this manner, Gompers sought, through Iglesias, to bring added pressure against the remaining recalcitrants on the island to support his position.

In his letter of May 11, Gompers refused to grant any authorization for a strike on the grounds that the primary task before the workers was to win the war against autocracy and for democracy, a task that vitally concerned all workingmen, and since a strike would hinder this effort, it could not be condoned.[51] To achieve justice for the workers, Gompers vowed to bring their plight before the president of the United States and the War Labor Board. Gompers struggled valiantly, on a political level, to get relief for the Puerto Rican workers. But he relied so heavily on government action and so little on the strength and militancy of the workingman that the slow workings of the federal bureaucracy eventually resulted in negligible relief to the workers. This cost the AFL the support of many of the workingmen of this Caribbean island. It gained the esteem of those who held prestigious positions in society, and suffered proportionately in the eyes of those who constituted its potential membership.

In spite of Gompers's monumental efforts to pacify labor during

49. J. Santos Rodriguez to Gompers, April 9, 1918, Gompers MSS.
50. *Ibid.*
51. Gompers to Santiago Iglesias, May 11, 1918, Gompers MSS.

the war, disaffection with the Federation's economic policies remained constant and unremitting. Workers expressed their discontent by engaging in more strike activity during the period than in any previous period of similar length in the history of the United States. During the years 1917 to 1918, approximately 4,000,000 workers were involved in strikes.[52] The combined efforts of the government and the Federation did little to ease the agitation. After nearly a year of war, *The New Republic* was still concerned with the mounting unrest in labor and the abnormal number of strikes, which kept occurring with "dangerous frequency."[53] In July, Senator Thomas of Colorado was telling the president that he was disturbed over the labor situation, which he thought was getting worse.[54] Questioning his Secretary of Labor, President Wilson received a more optimistic picture.[55] However, two months before the end of the war, Wilson was writing that "the complexities of the labor situation are multiplying rather than decreasing. . . ."[56]

Because of the never-ending labor turmoil, Wehle felt certain that had the war continued into 1919, some form of compulsion would have been resorted to.[57] In short, there is adequate evidence that a significant number of national unions, officials, and workers were not willing to accept the concept of an identity of interest between management, government, and labor. However, this feeling was strongly held during the early stages of the war and gradually began to diminish proportionately as conditions of labor began to improve, particularly during the last few months of war.

Although some labor disturbances were the result of disillusionment with the war, the overwhelming majority of strikes were due directly to economic causes and only indirectly to a spirit of protest against the war. Gompers's undeviating support of the Wilson Administration's domestic and foreign policies was not resulting in

---

52. Bing, *War Time Strikes,* pp. 156, 293. For comments on the effect of strikes during the initial phase of United States involvement see *New York Times,* August 5, 1917 (VI), pp. 6-7; and *Literary Digest* (November 24, 1917), pp. 14-15.
53. *The New Republic* (February 16, 1918), pp. 73-74.
54. Baker, *Woodrow Wilson: Life and Letters,* 8: 297.
55. *Ibid.*
56. Woodrow Wilson to Bainbridge Colby, September 16, 1918, Baker, *Woodrow Wilson: Life and Letters,* 8:407.
57. Wehle, *Hidden Threads,* p. 60.

substantial improvement in working conditions. This was not only a conclusion reached through a post-mortem examination of statistics, but was common knowledge at the time and recognized as such by some government officials and union leaders.

Although the war years of 1917-18 created a tremendous demand for labor, real wages did not rise uniformly for all wage earners. In many instances, sharp rises in the cost of living negated increases in money wages. Surprisingly, as a group, the unskilled nonunion worker fared better than the skilled worker who was a member of a trade union. Using 1914 as the base year, real wages for unskilled workers advanced 6 percent in 1916, remained the same in 1917, and rose a startling 19 percent in 1918.[58] On the other hand, real wages in union manufacturing industries and the building trades decreased by 21 percent in 1916, by 13 percent in 1917, and by 18 percent in 1918.[59] Real earnings in all manufacturing industries, again using 1914 as the base year, increased by 5 percent in 1916; by only 4 percent in 1917, a decrease of 1 percent from the last peacetime year; and by 8 percent in 1918.[60] Considering that in 1914 the economy was in a depressed state and that the wartime years represented a period of peak production and demand for labor, the welfare of the wages earners did not increase proportionately to the increase in the state of the economy.

Bernard Baruch, chairman of the War Industries Board, noted during the war that "with the exception of the sacrifices of the men in the armed services the greatest sacrifices have come from those at the lower wing of the industrial ladder. Wage increases respond last to the needs of this class."[61] At the other end of the economic spectrum, the Duluth *Labor Herald* acknowledged that labor was not being paid a living wage and that profits were piling up tremendously but, in line with Gompers's policies, the labor paper cautioned against any interruption of production, citing the winning of the war as basic to the future of democracy and the welfare of the

58. Paul H. Douglas, *Real Wages in the United States, 1890-1926* (Boston and New York: Houghton Mifflin Company, 1930), pp. 177-78.

59. *Ibid.*, p. 140.
60. *Ibid.*, p. 239.
61. Quoted in Coit, *Mr. Baruch*, p. 203.

workingman.[62] A close associate of Gompers during the war years and his advisor on foreign policy, pro-war socialist William English Walling, agreed that labor was "paying more for the war proportionately than any other class."[63] But, continued Walling, echoing Gompers's optimistic forecasts of the future, "war taxes and high prices are temporary and labor's gains are permanent."[64] Such was the rationale behind the Federation's domestic and foreign policies.

Part of the responsibility for the workingman's inability to improve substantially his position grew out of the Federation's abnormal involvement with foreign-policy issues and its myopic view of what was best for labor. Gompers's domestic program was subordinated to the government's needs, with the result that the Federation became more of an agency for the government than an advocate of the working class. The transition of the AFL from an outspoken interest group to a part of the administrative machinery of government was noted at the time and became the subject of several magazine articles and newspaper reports.[65] Its effect on Gompers can best be seen by observing those he worked with within the government, and watching his supporters and critics in the labor movement.

Dr. Franklin H. Martin, along with Gompers a member of the Advisory Commission since its inception, writes in a laudatory manner of the high degree of patriotism and loyalty to country that marked Gompers's work on the CND. What is of greater significance was the impression Martin retained of the extent to which Gompers was willing to sacrifice all in the name of patriotism. Gompers was prepared to tell his membership, Martin writes, "that they should disregard their unions if it was necessary to do so to serve their country better; in fact, to relinquish, if occasion required, everything that they had gained by organization in the last half century that had for

---

62. Cited by *Literary Digest* (November 24, 1917), pp. 4-5. The paper went on to label the calling of a strike without, at least, giving the government an opportunity to settle the grievance through conciliation, as akin to treason. Since bureaucratic procedures were extraordinarily slow, concilliation often led to an aggravation of the problem.
63. Cited by *Machinists' Monthly Journal* 30 (February 1918): 152.
64. *Ibid.*
65. *The New Republic* (June 8, 1918) pp. 164-66; *The Nation* (June 29, 1918), pp. 753-55; *Seamen's Journal* (July 3, 1918).

its object the betterment of their social and industrial conditions.''[66] While the statement may be a bit overdrawn, it was reflective of Gompers's general approach and willingness to sacrifice labor's gains for the sake of the larger interest—victory in the struggle against autocracy and for democracy.

Adverse reaction to the government's and Gompers's economic policies made labor unrest one of the most talked-about topics during the war. Many of the meetings of the Advisory Commission were opened with the words "labor again."[67] Labor dissatisfaction eventually led to a gradual erosion of the foundation upon which the unity of the Wilson Administration and Federation was built. Unions began to question the results of the AFL's March 12 Conference. In the process, a better understanding of the national and international union's support of the Administration's foreign policies was revealed.

Six months after the United States entered the war, the Painters' Union voiced its bitter disappointment over the lack of improvement in working conditions. The union disclosed some of the misgivings it and other national unions had about the Washington conference of March 12. They had assented to the document it produced on the premise that President Wilson and the cabinet would appreciate the services proferred and, in turn, would reciprocate.[68] However, their fears that subordinate officials in Washington would ignore "this informal but morally binding agreement" were now materializing.[69] The huge federal bureaucracy was proving unfriendly to organized labor and deliberately sabotaging any measure that might be of benefit to the workingman. Thus the Painters were raising a pointed question: Why should organized labor support the foreign policies of the Wilson Administration if this support did not, in turn, lead to greatly increased benefits to its membership?

The Painters were not alone in their skepticism. Sidney Hillman was appalled at the willingness of the AFL to sacrifice standards won

66. Franklin H. Martin, "Personal Reminiscences of Samuel Gompers," enclosed in a letter from Martin to John P. Frey, May 16, 1928, Frey MSS.
67. Franklin H. Martin, *Digest of the Proceedings of the Council of National Defense During the War* (Washington, D.C.: United States Government Printing Office, 1934), p. 346.
68. *The Painter and Decorator* 31 (August 1917): 420-21.
69. *Ibid.*
70. *Advance* (April 13, 1917).

through hard struggles.[70] Andrew Furuseth, leader of the Sailors' Union, opposed Gompers's general philosophy of labor passivity and lack of struggle, and declared that if organized labor "cannot get decent treatment while the war is yet on, we know what we are going to get when it is over and we might as well die raising hell as crawling on our knees with our forehead to the ground."[71]

Unions were also becoming concerned with the use of patriotism as a weapon to evade union standards and working conditions. At the outset of the war, the Electrical Workers' Union was already warning that patriotism "did not demand that men sacrifice the conditions fought for and obtained in the past. . . ."[72] Protesting their loyalty to the country, the railroad workers emphasized that patriotism did not "rest solely on [their] willingness to sacrifice [their] economic welfare unnecessarily for the benefit of [their] employer."[73] The union held fast to the principle that both the employer and the employee must sacrifice equally.

Writers favoring big business had, by 1918, come to the conclusion that the biggest threat to industrial peace did not arise from the socialists or pacifists, but from "the union fanatics who are devoted, above everything else, to the cause of organized labor."[74] These men, such authors complained, were more interested in winning the industrial war than the war against Germany. It was from this group of "union fanatics" that intense opposition developed to Gompers's tie with the government and its resultant policies on labor relations. Imbued with the spirit of trade unionism and fearful that the union cause was being undermined in the name of patriotism, a sizable number of trade-union officials were to pose a serious threat to Gompers's policies at the forthcoming convention of the AFL.

The 1917 AFL convention was historic, for it marked the first time a president of the United States ever addressed such a body of labor. Wilson's presence was deemed advantageous to both Gompers and the government. Gompers desired Wilson's attendance as a counter-

71. Furuseth to John Tennison, October 19, 1918, cited by Hyman Weintraub, *Andrew Furuseth: Emancipator of the Seamen* (Berkeley and Los Angeles: University of California Press, 1959), p. 149.
72. *Journal of Electrical Workers and Operators* 16 (April 1917): 551.
73. *The Railroad Trainman* 24 (September 1917): 657.
74. Burton J. Henrick, "The Leadership of Samuel Gompers," *World's Work* 35 (February 1918): 383-84.

weight to the voices of criticism and dissent expected to be raised against his policies.[75] The government, on the other hand, feared that the convention might adopt an "inelastic policy on labor relations which would complicate the government's task of composing differences between capital and labor."[76]

Concern by the Wilson Administration that the convention would take a hard line on "bread and butter" issues was well founded.[77] Dissatisfaction with the rising cost of living and the slow rate of wage increases ran across the entire gamut of labor officialdom. Although Gompers easily won reelection, the defeat of John B. Lennon by Daniel J. Tobin was widely regarded as a defeat of a steadfast Gompers supporter by a man whose enthusiasm for the war was considered lukewarm.[78]

Faced with growing opposition to his policies and unwilling to take any affirmative action that might jeopardize his arrangements with the government, Gompers was forced more and more to rely on government action to help solve some of the erupting industrial problems. But the vast bureaucracy that made up the lower echelons of government were not always willing to implement with good faith what was decided on in Washington, while the upper layers of officialdom were either too busy, too reluctant, or powerless to have their decisions implemented. Caught in such uncomfortable circumstances, Gompers often sought to spur Washington into taking effective action by raising the terrifying possibility that, if concessions were not made to him, his influence would be greatly diminished and his following would gradually drift into the camp of the pacifists and socialists.[79]

If Gompers sought to frighten government and management into

75. *The Tailor* 6 (November 1917): 7.
76. Newton D. Baker to Woodrow Wilson, October 18, 1917, Baker MSS. Baker was not concerned over Gompers's position but was worried about what might happen in the heat of a convention. In comparing the attitude of capital and labor he was to write that in his "own dealing with the industrial problems here, [he] . . . found labor more willing to keep step than capital." See Baker to Woodrow Wilson, November 10, 1917, Baker MSS.
77. *Coast Seamen's Journal* (November 21, 1917). Labor reporter Laurence Todd gives an excellent description of the various forces moving to undercut Gompers's position.
78. *World's Work* 35 (January, 1918): 233.
79. Gompers to Thomas W. Gregory, January 19, 1918, Gompers MSS; E. David Cronon, ed., *The Cabinet Diaries of Josephus Daniels, 1913-1921* (Lincoln: University of Nebraska Press, 1963), p. 196.

concessions by raising the "specter of communism," Wilson, in support of Gompers, let it be known that his backing of labor was contingent on its support of Gompers and the Administration's policies. When the Texas Federation of Labor voiced its concern over the activities of anti-union elements, Wilson assured the group it would be protected from its enemies so long as the workers pursued the loyal and patriotic couse laid down by the Federation.[80]

As the war drew to a close, Gompers grew ever more confident that the policies he pursued were best for labor and that the coming years would prove their productiveness. He was now at the zenith of his power and recognized as a world statesman. He was proud as he recalled labor's wartime gains: recognition by the government of organized labor's right to organize and bargain collectively; a union membership that had more than doubled; a virtual state of full employment; and above all, his close personal relationship with President Wilson that remained unimpaired. Still, voices of caution began to be heard. The total reliance of the AFL on President Wilson, and its failure to consolidate wartime gains and make the Federation more impregnable to attack were questioned in view of the shifting political winds, which might place in the White House a successor unfriendly to labor.[81]

But the logic behind this analysis did not move Gompers. Neither was he impressed with a survey of labor's political influence, as reported by a pro-labor journalist, showing that in the making of national legislation in the coming years the American labor movement had less influence than the labor movement of any other major nation.[82]

Gompers remained unperturbed, soothed by his own philosophy that the war was bringing about a new social era that would recognize the labor movement as a vital factor on the industrial scene. In the years to come, "labor statesmanship" was to become a euphemism applied to those labor leaders who sacrificed their membership's welfare in order to be extolled and praised by the leaders of society.

80. Woodrow Wilson to G. H. Slater, March 26, 1918, Baker, *Woodrow Wilson, Life and Letters*, 8: 54-55.
81. *Advance* (June 14, 1918).
82. *Seamen's Journal* (October 30, 1918).

8

Labor and Military Mobilization

Gompers's aim of making organized labor accepted as a respected part of the American scene included a serious attempt to moderate the abrasive relations that had existed between labor and other important institutions of the state—especially the military. Any objective that envisioned a close working relationship between the armed forces and the labor movement was bound to encounter serious obstacles. So often had the army been used as an instrument to thwart labor's legitimate desires that it awoke in the average workingman an automatic reaction of hatred against anything associated with it. Such events were not only relics of a bygone era, but recurred frequently enough to remind labor of the role of its traditional enemies. Even during the war, when organized labor's aid was welcomed by all agencies of the government, the army reverted to its old role of strikebreaking. Its intervention in an industrial dispute in Newark, New Jersey, was terminated only by the action of the Secretary of War, who was concerned that the activity of the troops might prejudice labor's attitude toward the war.[1]

1. Newton D. Baker to Gompers, June 5, 1917, Gompers MSS. Baker's response reflects government concern with labor's attitude toward the war: ". . .in these days. . .," wrote Baker, "it is essential that the military be esteemed in the eyes of labor, for what it is in fact, as representative of the citizenry of the whole people."

Gompers faced one of his most difficult problems over the question of raising a large army through universal military service. Founded on the philosophy of voluntarism as opposed to compulsion, the Federation could hardly support a program that was at variance with its basic ideology. Seeking to please the government and, at the same time, fearing to go against the obvious wishes of his membership, Gompers adopted a dual approach. His public statements were outright attacks on any military program making use of compulsory military service while, behind the scenes, he was a prime influence in moving the Administration to propose such a program to Congress. It was a classical example of the manner in which the president of the AFL utilized his organization to influence the decision-making process of government in a way obviously contrary to the wishes of his membership.

The issue of compulsory military service created a sharp division within Gompers's own circle of supporters. A serious argument erupted in the Executive Council as to whether the Federation would support compulsion, not only during the present conflict, but as a permanent institution in American life.[2] A majority of the Council opposed any such policy. But the debate was sharp and acrimonious, with Gompers siding against the majority. Since, constitutionally, the Executive Council was the highest body between conventions, its decisions were binding on all officials of the AFL. But a degree of nervousness began to infect many of the members of the Council in their anticipation of what Gompers would do.[3] So vehement was Gompers in favor of compulsion, that the impression grew among Council members that he would commit the Federation to a course of action to which the majority was opposed. Cognizant of the agitation and uncertainty over what he might do, Gompers sought to reassure

---

2. *Official Magazine—Teamsters* 14 (April 1917): 10-11. In a biting comment about those labor officials who favored military compulsion on the Council, Tobin wrote that there were many who still "like to hear brass bands play and the drums roll around their own names."

3. *Coast Seamen's Journal* (April 4, 1917). Reports were already circulating that Gompers would declare in favor of compulsion. In an editorial, the Sailor's Union declared that in any such declaration Gompers spoke only for himself and had no authority to commit the labor movement. Furthermore, the *Journal* believed "that a referendum of the A.F. of L. membership . . . would give a substantial majority against Mr. Gompers' alleged declaration."

the Council members. On March 23, he wrote one of his most ardent supporters and trusted lieutenants, First Vice-President James Duncan, that he would "do nothing by word or act in advocacy of universal military service . . . until after mature discussion with you and the other associate members of the Council."[4] Gompers went on to pledge that as an organization man he would voluntarily submit to the discipline expected of him.[5] How well Gompers submitted himself to organizational discipline now becomes a matter of dispute.

On March 24, at a joint meeting of the Advisory Commission and the Council of National Defense, Chairman Willard declared that "the members of the Commission were, individually, all for universal military service, but that the Commission as a whole had not recommended its adoption because of the position in which one of its members [Gompers] was personally placed."[6] The Commission went on to recommend the raising of 1,000,000 men for the army and bringing the navy to full wartime strength.[7]

At the same meeting, in explanation of labor's position, Secretary of Labor Wilson stated that Gompers was for universal service but his organization was not. Furthermore, the Secretary continued, if Gompers should announce his support for compulsory military service, he might defeat its adoption by his organization.[8] In the interest of expediency no vote was taken, "but the Secretary of War was authorized to interpret the Commission's views to the President."[9] Thus Gompers avoided formally committing himself, but President Wilson could not help but be impressed by the fact that if he advocated universal military service, Gompers would be able to dilute labor's antagonism and its opposition would be lukewarm at most. It would not be inappropriate to draw the conclusion that Gompers violated the spirit of his pledge to do nothing by "word or act" in favor of compulsory military service.

4. Gompers to James Duncan, March 23, 1917, Gompers MSS.
5. *Ibid.*
6. Franklin H. Martin, *Digest of the Proceedings of the Council of National Defense During the War* (Washington, D.C.: United States Government Printing Office, 1934), p. 112.
7. Grosvenor B. Clarkson, *Industrial America in the World War* (Boston & New York: Houghton Mifflin Company, 1924), p. 32.
8. Martin, *Digest of Proceedings,* p. 112.
9. Clarkson, *Industrial America,* p. 92.

Although favoring universal military service in the inner councils of government, Gompers publicly campaigned against its adoption. In letters, speeches, and before the House Military Affairs Committee, Gompers supported labor's traditional adherence to voluntary institutions as opposed to compulsory legislation.[10]

In his Autobiography, Gompers was to confess to his unauthorized behavior. He candidly admitted he "assumed responsibility as representative of labor on the Advisory Commission of cooperating in the development of plans for the draft."[11] He justified his action on the basis of his uncanny foresight: "I knew that this draft was in harmony with the principles of organized labor and that organized labor, after it had the opportunity to consider the new situation would approve the policy."[12] It was a revealing example of how the president of the AFL was almost single-handedly able to mold Federation policy in the realm of defense and foreign affairs.

As millions of Americans were being drafted into the army, Gompers became concerned with established procedures for officer recruitment. He was critical of the system because it placed such great emphasis upon college training and narrowed the choice of officer material to a few select groups. Gompers was interested in democratizing the army and believed this goal could best be reached by making commissioned and noncommissioned ranks open to broader sections of the population. He saw a vast reservoir of competent officer material among the many shop foremen, shop stewards, tradeunion officials, and other natural leaders of the workingmen. Gompers went so far as to suggest that soldiers elect the officers to be in immediate command of them.[13] Although he was persistent in his

10. After the joint meeting of the Advisory Commission and CND on March 24, Gompers kept up a running fire against compulsory service. On April 17, he wrote that since voluntary principles guided industrial organization, it "must be the initial basic principle in the military." See Gompers to John W. Rogers, April 17, 1917, Gompers MSS. On April 27, he supported this view before the Senate. See Executive Council to Thomas R. Marshall, April 27, 1917, Gompers MSS. For further examples of Gompers's and the Executive Council's public statements, see Samuel Gompers, *American Labor and the War* (New York: George H. Doran Company, 1919), p. 149; AFL, *Proceedings* (1917), pp. 72, 112.
11. Samuel Gompers, *Seventy Years of Life and Labor* (New York: E. P. Dutton and Company, 1925), 2: 369.
12. *Ibid.*
13. Gompers to Newton D. Baker, June 12, 1917, Gompers MSS; Memorandum for the Secretary of War from W. L., June 16, 1917, Baker MSS.

demand, the response from the War Department was less than enthusiastic. Three weeks after making his recommendations, Gompers had still not received a reply from Secretary of War Baker. Again taking pen in hand, Gompers requested the War Department to give special consideration to qualified labor men who may have been lacking in some technical qualifications, but not in overall competence and ability.[14]

With the passage of universal military training into law, organized labor turned its attention to the system of drafting millions of Americans into the armed forces. At the heart of the system were the draft boards and their power to determine exemptions. Gompers demanded that wage earners be represented on every board—national, state, and local—that was responsible for administering the law.[15] Of prime importance to labor was the power of these boards to determine fitness for military and industrial service. Gompers was anxious that representatives of labor be appointed to District Exemption Boards, which had the power to review decisions in all exemption cases made by lower bodies and which had direct jurisdiction in industrial cases. As a result of his efforts, Gompers was able to obtain the agreement of the appropriate authorities to name a representative list of labor men to sit in several federal judicial districts to determine claims for exemption from military service.[16]

Gompers's Committee on Labor of the Advisory Commission was a largely inactive and ineffectual body throughout the war. It was accorded few tasks to perform and even its one piece of major innovation and activity—a bill for family allowances and compensation of injured soldiers and sailors—was eventually taken from it.

Gompers originally proposed the idea to President Wilson, who suggested that he discuss it with others.[17] It was presented by Gompers to the CND, where the suggestion that it be worked upon by the Committee on Labor was approved.[18] The Committee enlisted the aid

14. Gompers to Newton D. Baker, July 12, 1917, Gompers MSS.
15. AFL, *Weekly News Letter* (May 26, 1917).
16. Gompers to General Crowder, June 18, 1917, Gompers MSS.; Gompers, *Seventy Years*, 2:370; AFL, *Proceedings* (1917), p. 81.
17. Woodrow Wilson to Gompers, April 19, 1917. Ray Stannard Baker, *Woodrow Wilson: Life and Letters* (New York: Doubleday, Doran and Company, 1939), 7:29.
18. AFL, *Proceedings* (1917), pp. 79-80.

of Judge Julien W. Mack to draw up a draft of the bill. At a point when the work was almost completed, Secretary of the Treasury McAdoo conceived of the same idea and began to work on it. Discovering Gompers's plans, McAdoo requested that he be allowed to present the bill first and make the necessary recommendations to President Wilson before Gompers presented it to the CND. Gompers agreed.[19] Secretary of War Baker was subsequently to confirm Gompers's authorship of this particular piece of legislation and call it "the greatest single service Mr. Gompers performed during the War. . . ."[20]

One of the foremost problems facing American industry as it geared itself to wartime production was the proper supply and allocation of manpower. Priority was to be given to those firms whose products were essential to the war effort. Since the government lacked any overall plan to deal with the problem, serious shortages began to develop in certain areas. A debate soon erupted as to the cause and solution of the problem. Employers were convinced that the nation faced an actual shortage in the supply of manpower and, if the difficulty was to be resolved quickly, the government would have to resort to some plan involving the conscription of labor. The AFL, on the other hand, held to the belief that the alleged shortage of labor was due mainly to the improper allocation of manpower, and that the best method of dealing with the crisis was to establish a national employment bureau equipped to give the necessary information to labor and management.

The earliest proposal involving the distribution of labor called for the organization of an "industrial reserve." It sought to place all industrial manpower under the control of the military, who would have the power to allocate labor where needed, including the right to transfer employees from one location to another. The AFL opposed such an experiment because of its military features but recognized the necessity of adopting some plan that would meet the needs of a wartime economy.[21]

The continued misplacement and dislocation of labor was ample

19. Gompers to Newton D. Baker, July 26, 1917, Baker MSS.
20. Baker to John P. Frey, December 6, 1926, Frey MSS.
21. AFL, *Proceedings* (1917), p. 89.

testimony to the fact that the Employment Service as well as other government-related agencies were not adequate to meet the demands being placed upon them. Attention was again centered on establishing some form of labor conscription. On May 17, 1918, Provost Marshal General Enoch H. Crowder promulgated an amendment to the Selective Service Regulations based on the principle of "Work or Fight." The new regulation applied to those men who were in a deferred classification and were either unemployed or employed at occupations not considered essential to the war effort. Hereafter, to be exempt from military service, the potential draftee had to be employed at work considered productive.

Of utmost importance to organized labor was the question of whether the order was meant to bring all industrial workers under military control, and its potential use in labor disturbances. If a worker on strike could be classified as an idler and subjected to induction into the army, then labor would be robbed of its most effective weapon and its activities severely curtailed. On these most important subjects, the regulation was silent. As a result, the fear that the amendment could be utilized for anti-labor purposes, as well as a reluctance to establish such a dangerous precedent, led some unionists to oppose it.[22]

To allay labor's concern, Secretary of War Baker issued a statement clarifying the views of the War Department. The new amendment to the draft was interpreted as having no effect on the relations between management and labor. Baker also emphasized the intention of the Administration not to apply the draft regulation in the event of a strike.[23] President Wilson underscored the views of his secretary of war and was convinced that labor's apprehension was the result of a misunderstanding.[24] Gompers, assured by the Wilson Administration that it did not intend to put labor under military control and yielding to the patriotic appeal of the crisis, ceased his opposition to the measure.[25]

---

22. John Lombardi, *Labor's Voice in the Cabinet* (New York: Columbia University Press, 1942), p. 186.
23. *New York Times,* May 28, 1918, p. 14.
24. Woodrow Wilson to Secretary Baker, August 20, 1918, Baker, *Woodrow Wilson: Life and Letters,* 8:346-47.
25. *American Federationist* 25 (July 1918): 595-97.

Through its activity in behalf of the armed forces, the AFL attempted to form a close working relationship with the military establishment. The failure of this relationship to fully bloom in the coming years was due entirely to the hostility of elements within the army, and not to any unwillingness on the part of the AFL.[26]

26. The beginnings of this relationship can now be firmly established through the use of documents in Frey MSS. See also James O. Morris, *Conflict Within the AFL* (Ithaca, New York: Cornell University Press, 1958), pp. 71-81.

9

Labor and the War of Words

Unquestionably, large numbers of workers were alienated from supporting the war because of the failure of their unions and the government to improve markedly their working conditions. In addition, substantial groups of workers also opposed the war because of ideological reasons, convinced that the conflict was a rich man's war with the workingman merely a pawn in a game from which he would reap little gain, whoever the victor. Eventually, both groups were to coalesce in a common effort.

The failure of the average workingman to give his wholehearted support to the war effort was recognized by industrial leaders, trade-union officials, and the Wilson Administration. Fully convinced that Ludendorff was correct in his oft-repeated statement that victory in modern-day warfare was no longer won by the soldiers in the field but depended mainly on the morale of all the people, the United States government organized a Committee on Public Information to coordinate all propaganda and publicity during the war. One of its prime objects was to increase labor productivity by counteracting anti-war sentiment in the factories and raising the level of patriotic fervor. To head the agency, President Wilson selected George Creel, a celebrated journalist with impeccable liberal credentials. The choice of a liberal was not accidental. Wilson was concerned lest a growing peace movement recruit into its ranks a considerable number of workers, particularly the skilled craftsmen, sufficient to disrupt those inner lines that were so essential to the maintenance of a successful war effort. Creel, with contacts in both groups, was regarded as a

136

logical choice to persuade pacifists and labor of the lofty ideals for which the war was being fought.

As the work of the CPI developed, the struggle to hold labor's loyalty occupied much of its time. In this effort, it was to obtain the unlimited cooperation of the AFL, as well as that of all associations representing management.

As the realization that America had finally entered the conflict slowly dawned on the American people, opponents of the war began to create an organizational instrument to give voice to their opposition. Coalescing around a broad demand for a negotiated peace and the protection of worker's rights during wartime, a coalition of anti-war groups and socialists joined together in May 1917 to hold the First American Conference for Democracy and Terms of Peace. Issuing the call for its first meeting in New York City were officials from some of the leading trade unions in the country, particularly those centered in New York City with a large membership in the garment trades.[1] Also supporting the call was Judge Jacob Panken, Rabbi Judah Magnes and Morris Hillquit of the Socialist Party. The result of the conference was the formation of a permanent organization, the People's Council for Democracy and Terms of Peace. It was also decided that the newly formed People's Council would hold its first national convention during the month of September in Minneapolis.

The program of the People's Council placed it in direct opposition to the policies pursued by the Wilson Administration and the AFL. It called for the Allied governments to state concretely the terms on which they would be willing to make peace, based upon the principles of ''(a) no forcible annexations (b) no punitive indemnities [and] (c) free development for all nationalities''; opposition to conscription; the preservation of democratic liberties within the country; and the

---

1. *Advance* (May 25, 1917). The most prominent were Joseph Schlossberg, secretary, Amalgamated Clothing Workers of America; Abraham Baroff, secretary-treasurer of the International Ladies' Garment Workers' Union; James H. Maurer, president of the Pennsylvania State Federation of Labor; Rose Schneidermann of the New York Women's Trade Union League; and Mary Kenny O'Sullivan, organizer for the AFL and representative of various teacher unions.

safeguarding of labor standards.[2] To implement the last, the Council's economic program called for the financial burden of the war to be met by placing progressively higher taxes on the wealthy and for a reduction in the high cost of living. The platform of the People's Council sought to link the issue of peace with the economic welfare of the workingman. The Council viewed the war as a conflict not for the right of self-determination of all peoples but for imperial expansion and economic gain. If this was the objective of United States policy overseas, under a government the Council regarded as manipulated by the capitalist class, then, the Council reasoned, the government's domestic policy would complement its foreign policy, with the result that worker rights at home would be suppressed under the guise of patriotism and loyalty. Thus, the foreign and domestic program of President Wilson was viewed by the Council as intertwined with and in the service of those who profited most from war. It was a platform designed to appeal to labor.

During the summer months, as Council propaganda spread throughout the country, it was becoming apparent that the anti-war movement was making considerable headway among the American people. By June, President Wilson was sufficiently aroused to speak out in behalf of his policies and to condemn pacifist propaganda. To Wilson, those who advocated peace no longer manifested a mistaken judgement, but were engaged in a sinister intrigue on behalf of Germany to divide the American people. The president equated the advocacy of peace with treason.[3] It was not a particularly instructive lesson to Samuel Gompers. He had formulated just such a public position long before its adoption by the president of the United States.

Shortly afterwards, Gompers began to receive alarming reports about the success of the People's Council in trade-union circles, particularly in New York City. The attitude of labor was of special con-

2. Reports of First American Conference for Democracy and Terms of Peace, New York City, May 30 and 31, 1917, may be found in People's Council Manuscripts, Tamiment Library, New York City.
3. Wilson's Flag Day address, June 14, 1917, in Albert Shaw, ed., *The Messages and Papers of Woodrow Wilson* (New York: The Review of Reviews Corporation, 1924), 1:415-18.

cern to both Wilson and Gompers, since the success of the anti-war drive was dependent on its ability to attract labor to its cause.

The rapid growth of anti-war sentiment and the favorable response it received from labor surprised both its organizers and the Federation leadership. It was acknowledged that, scarcely a month after it came into existence, the Council had greater strength and financial backing than any peace group formed since the war.[4]

To facilitate its working among trade unionists, the Council organized a separate unit known as the Workmen's Division. It was to be affiliated with the parent body, but its sole area of concentration was to propagandize among labor. In some areas, it was known as the Workmen's Council. By August, the Workmen's Council embraced the entire United Hebrew Trades numbering 250,000 men and women affiliated with the AFL together with 64 local unions among the ILGWU, Painters', Carpenters', Jewelers', and Bakers' Unions.[5] In Boston, approximately 100 locals joined its ranks.[6] Cigar workers organized themselves in the Progressive Cigar Makers' Union and held a joint meeting with the Council to denounce the Wilson Administration.[7] The Furriers' Joint Board, although voting not to send a delegate to the first conference of the People's Council, decided to endorse its principles and politics. The Furriers claimed that 500,000 members of the AFL were affiliated with the Council. The influence of the Council among New York City wage earners was regarded by the AFL leadership as critical.[8] A mood of apprehension was overtaking Gompers, who worried that the workers of New York City "would become alienated from the best interests of America and from cooperation with American workers."[9] Adding to Gompers's concern were activities on the West Coast, where the Seamen's Union, in support of the People's Council, voiced the hope that it would receive "a more enthusiastic reception at the coming AFL convention than it did in the Executive Council of AFL."[10]

4. *New York Times,* July 1, 1917, p. 12.
5. *The Survey* (August 4, 1917), p. 411.
6. *Ibid.*
7. *New York Times,* August 20, 1917, p. 4.
8. *The Fur Worker* 6 (August 1917).
9. AFL, *Proceedings* (1917), p. 95.
10. *Coast Seamen's Journal* (August 8, 1917).

Toward the middle of August, the Council, in an optimistic mood, issued a statement claiming that a new local union of the AFL was joining it each day, and projecting a membership of two million by September, which would be made up largely of AFL members.[11] While the Council figures may have been slightly exaggerated, it was receiving support from a cross-section of American labor to a degree that caused Gompers to term the "situation dangerous," and to seek an organizational alternative.[12]

Particularly distasteful to Gompers was that part of the program of the People's Council which called on all the belligerents publicly to state their war aims and to amplify the terms upon which they would be willing to make peace. But of overriding concern to the Federation leaders was the charge by the Council that workers' rights were not being protected during the war and its statement that a campaign to safeguard working conditions would have to be waged by it due to the abdication of such a role by the AFL.

The Council played upon the theme that the war aims of the Allied powers were purposely obscured because its statesmen harbored designs not in keeping with their openly proclaimed democratic objectives. This feeling was also privately voiced by some in Gompers's inner circle, who questioned whether the Allies were in earnest in their advocacy of political democracy and social justice.[13] While the People's Council favored the publication of the nation's war aims, the AFL took the opposite approach and counseled against the formulation of specific peace terms until the Central powers agreed to unconditional surrender.[14]

To forestall mounting criticism of its position, the AFL adopted a set of five principles to be used as standards in the writing of any peace treaty.[15] The principles set forth by the Federation failed to

11. *New York Times,* August 16, 1917, p. 6.
12. Samuel Gompers, *Seventy Years of Life and Labor* (New York: E. P. Dutton and Company, 1925), 2:382.
13. John B. Lennon to Walsh, May 7, 1917, Walsh MSS.
14. AFL, *Proceedings* (1918), p. 337. See also *American Socialist* (September 8, 1917), where this position was criticized by the Seamen's Union.
15. AFL, *Proceedings* (1918), pp. 53-4. The list of principles follows:
    1. A league of the free peoples of the world in a common covenant for genuine and practical cooperation to secure justice and therefore peace in relations between nations.
    2. No political or economic restrictions meant to benefit some nations and to cripple or embarrass others.

meet the demand for specificity in delineating America's war aims, and were so general in character as to allow the victorious nations wide latitude in formulating their demands at the peace table. In response to the demand of "no annexations, no indemnities," the Federation limited its implementation by favoring "no indemnities . . . [except] to right manifest wrongs," and "no territorial changes . . . except . . . in furtherance of world peace." These qualifications were vague enough so as to give the victorious powers a free hand in revamping the map of Europe. It provided little comfort for those who were opposed to a punitive peace settlement. It was also reminiscent of the language of the Wilson Administration, whose war aims were couched in such terms as "right . . . justice and liberty."

The formation of the Workmen's Council was regarded by the AFL leadership as a threat not only to the Federation but to their own influence and power.[16] It was seen as a dual union, a separatist movement to split the workers away from the regular leadership.[17] With European labor divided over the issue of a negotiated peace, and the socialist trade-union forces in the ascendancy, Gompers could not lightly disregard the Council as just another movement of dreamers. The twin issues of peace and workers' rights were uniting groups that had heretofore found no common ground, and were threatening, in 1917, to lead European labor organizations in a direction contrary to the wishes of their respective governments. If the Federation was to persist in its policies, it would have to combat effectively the People's Council and its program.[18]

3. No indemnities or reprisals based upon vindictive purposes or deliberate desire to injure, but to right manifest wrongs.
4. Recognition of the rights of small nations and of the principle, "No people must be forced under sovereignty under which it does not wish to live."
5. No territorial changes or adjustment of power except in furtherance of the welfare of the peoples affected and in furtherance of world peace.
In addition to these basic principles, the AFL proposed that a set of declarations relating to wage earners be incorporated in the peace treaty.
16. AFL, *Proceedings* (1917), pp. 94-95; Gompers, "Labor and Democracy," *American Federationist* 24 (October 1917): 837-42.
17. Speech accepting presidency of American Alliance for Labor and Democracy, September 7, 1917, in Samuel Gompers, *American Labor and the War* (New York: George H. Doran Company, 1919), pp. 114-15; AFL, *Proceedings* (1918). p. 5.
18. Gompers, *Seventy Years,* 2:401.

The Federation sought its answer in the formation of the American Alliance for Labor and Democracy.

The AALD was organized on the initiative of Samuel Gompers. He first submitted the plan to the CND and to George Creel, who was appointed by Wilson as director of the Committee on Public Information.[19] During the latter part of July, Wilson gave his approval of the new organization. Creel promptly informed Gompers that he would have the support of the CPI in his "attempt to Americanize the labor movement."[20] Gompers's idea was to bring together two previously hostile elements—socialists who had left their party in order to support the war and the AFL leadership—into an organization that would support Woodrow Wilson's foreign policies and fight radicalism within the labor movement. It was to be nominally independent, but became, in fact, an auxiliary of the CPI, which was its main source of funds. If its original intention was to propagandize the American workingman, it eventually expanded its activities into foreign countries and became an instrument for carrying out United States foreign policy abroad. The Alliance was, in reality, a "front" for a large part of the government's work with labor.[21]

Although the Alliance was to be largely funded by the CPI, this was not acknowledged publicly. When the president of the Pennsylvania State Federation of Labor addressed an open letter to Gompers asking who was financing the Alliance, the head of the AFL indignantly refused to answer.[22] In other words, the general public was led to believe the AALD was an independent, self-sustaining organization.

The dual objectives of the Alliance soon became apparent in the pledge of loyalty all prospective members were required to take upon joining. Not only were they obliged to pledge their support of the

19. Stokes to Harriet Jones, October 24, 1917, James G. Phelps Stokes Papers, Butler Library, Columbia University, New York City; Gompers, *Seventy Years*, 3:381.
20. Creel to Gompers, July 26, 1917, cited by Frank L. Grubbs, Jr., *The Struggle for Labor Loyalty: Gompers, the A. F. of L., and the Pacifists, 1917-1920* (Durham, N.C.: Drake University Press, 1968), p. 44.
21. James R. Mock and Cedric Larson, *Words That Won The War* (Princeton: Princeton University Press, 1939), p. 191.
22. *New York Call*, October 7, 1917; *Social Revolution* (formerly "National Rip-Saw") (November 1917).

government's war policies, but they also had to affirm their loyalty to the AFL in its struggle against potential rivals.[23] In effect, federal funds were to be used to support a particular trade union and its philosophy against its opponents. This was to take concrete form when the IWW began to make inroads on AFL membership.

A respected labor journalist writing in the iconoclastic *Seamen's Journal* pictured the debate between the AALD and People's Council as determining more than just the direction and end of United States foreign policy. He saw it as also resolving the degree to which the membership of the AFL should take part in the framing of foreign policy.[24] Decades of practice led Gompers to favor procedures that placed the decision-making process in the hands of a small circle of leaders. This was particularly true in the field of foreign policy. The purpose of the Alliance was not to include the AFL membership in the process of formulating foreign policy, but to convince them of the soundness of the position of the AFL and of President Wilson's leadership. Thus the efforts of the People's Council threatened the tight control that leaders like Gompers held over the membership. By its own momentum, the struggle against the anti-war movement by the Federation leadership broadened itself into a struggle against further democratizing the administrative structure within the AFL.

Despite government backing and the wholehearted cooperation of the AFL bureaucracy, the Alliance failed to gain substantial broad-based support within the labor movement. Its opening convention at Minneapolis was to be a preview of its future strength and influence. Trade-union representation at the conference was disappointingly low. Out of 170 delegates who attended, 89 were trade unionists. Many of the trade-union delegates were from small federal labor unions and officials of the Federation itself. Few represented any of the large unions connected with war work.[25] Approximately half the delegates present represented various socialist groups, the major exception being the Minneapolis delegation, which was composed mostly

23. Gompers, *Seventy Years,* 2:383; Gompers to Robert Maisel, September 29, 1917, Stokes MSS; Robert Maisel's Report to Executive Council of AALD, February 20, 1918, Stokes MSS; Robert Maisel to George Creel, March 19, 1918, Committee on Public Information Files, 1-A1, National Archives, Washington, D.C.
24. *Coast Seamen's Journal* (September 12, 1917).
25. Lewis L. Lorwin, *The American Federation of Labor* (Washington, D.C.: Brookings Institution, 1933), p. 150.

of trade unionists.[26] This led some unions to object to the convention's adopting resolutions in the name of organized labor. An attitude gaining prominence among trade unionists was that the meeting was Gompers's own "personally conducted highbrow conference," which was not "competent to speak for the trade union movement. . . ."[27]

President Wilson was invited to address the convention. He did not appear in person but sent a letter to Gompers indicating his total support for the crusade against disloyalty. Wilson, sympathizing with the fears of the workers, recognized that "too often military necessities have been made an excuse for the destruction of laboriously-erected industrial and social standards." However, Wilson stressed, under his Administration such fears proved to be groundless. He offered the full support of the government in gaining for "the toiler a new dignity and new sense of social and economic security."[28] The cooperation between the pro-war socialists and the AFL over foreign-policy issues was to be of lasting significance to the labor movement. Their joint effort was to result in the beginnings of an international policy buttressed by a dedication to anti-communism which, at times, tended to obscure all other problems, and was to dominate completely AFL thinking until the present day.

Reaction to the Alliance consisted of a mixture of apathy and bitter opposition. It was endorsed by the AFL convention only after a prolonged and acrimonious debate.[29] Indicative of labor's lack of support was the reluctance of many unions to contribute financially to its fund-raising drives. Appeals by Gompers for funds met with a re-

26. Stokes to Gompers, October 16, 1917, Stokes MSS; John Spargo and Stokes to Members of the Social Democratic League, November 1, 1917, Stokes MSS.

27. *Coast Seamen's Journal* (September 26, 1917); *The Fur Worker* 6 (October 1917).

28. Woodrow Wilson to Gompers, August 31, 1917, Wilson MSS.

29. AFL, *Proceedings* (1917), pp. 283-308. The overwhelming vote—21,602 in favor, 402 opposed, and 1,305 not voting—supporting the AALD concealed the intensity and breadth of opposition to it. Matthew Woll was forced to appeal to the delegates on the basis that a rejection of the Alliance would be a repudiation of the entire leadership of the Federation and hence damaging to labor unity at this crucial time. See also Gompers's Report to Executive Council of AALD, February 21, 1918, Stokes MSS, in which the AFL chief describes the opposition as chiefly centered in the "Ladies' Garment Workers, the Cap-Makers and those who for some reason or other cast their lot against America."

sponse that fell far below expectations.[30] This made it increasingly difficult for the AALD to operate with any degree of independence and it became almost wholly dependent on the government for its survival.

Records of the Alliance indicate that it encountered intense hostility in the highly industrialized large city areas in the East among the Irish, German, and Austro-Hungarian ethnic groups, and in New York City where the East Side and the garment unions were virtual hotbeds of anti-war sentiment.[31] So strong was opposition to the government's policies among the Jewish population that the Alliance organized a special Jewish Department to combat it.[32] President Wilson was sufficiently concerned about the Jewish attitude to urge Clarence Darrow to work on the East Side in behalf of the government.[33] Anti-war sentiment among the foreign-born did not abate as the war dragged on, and in April 1918, we find officials of the Alliance complaining that the German membership of a large AFL union refused to attend a union ball because it was decided to give the affair a patriotic theme.[34]

In Chicago, work by the Alliance was at a standstill. The Chicago unions ignored its existence and would have nothing to do with its activities.[35] This was not unusual, since the Alliance found itself weakest in states where organized labor had considerable strength

---

30. Unsigned, undated note, CPI Files, 1-A6, National Archives. Gompers made his appeal on January 21, 1918, and by February 1, only $700 was collected. The writer noted the results as poor. For further information on financing of the Alliance, see Gompers to Robert Maisel, August 2, 1917, Gompers MSS; Stokes to Maisel, August 22, 1917, Stokes MSS; Director, Division of Business Management of CPI to Stokes, November 13, 1918, Stokes MSS.
31. *New York Times,* July 29, 1917, I, p. 9; Gertrude Barnum, "Russian-Americans and the Government," *American Federationist* 24 (August 1917): 631-33; Gompers, *Seventy Years,* 2: 379; Maisel to George Creel, May 3, 1918, 1-A1, CPI Files, National Archives; Colonel, General Staff, Chief, Military Intelligence Section to Newton D. Baker, November 23, 1917, Baker MSS.
32. Robert Maisel's Report to Executive Council of AALD, February 20, 1918, Stokes MSS.
33. Woodrow Wilson to Clarence S. Darrow, August 9. 1917, in Ray Stannard Baker, *Woodrow Wilson: Life and Letters* (Garden City, N.Y.: Doubleday, Doran and Company, 1939), 7:210.
34. *Machinist's Monthly Journal* 30 (April 1918): 343-44.
35. Minutes of Executive Council Meeting of AALD, February 21, 1918, Stokes MSS.

—New York, New Jersey, Connecticut, Pennsylvania, and Rhode Island.[36]

A crucial test of the Administration's wartime program was to take place in the off-year elections of November 1917. The main battle-ground was to be New York City, where Morris Hillquit, an avowed member of the Socialist Party and vehement critic of the war, was running for mayor on a peace ticket. Hilquit was endorsed by the ACWA, ILGWU, Neckwear Workers' Union, International Fur Workers' Union, and the United Hebrew Trades.[37] He was opposed by the AALD, whose treasurer, T. Phelps Stokes, admitted that the vote would be a test of war sentiment.[38]

The results astounded the nation. Hillquit polled 22 percent of the vote, carrying 12 election districts and electing 10 assemblymen and 7 aldermen on the Socialist ticket. The most warlike candidate, Mayor Mitchell, who lost the election to his Tammany foe, polled only 9,267 votes more than Hillquit. Injecting a note of realism into a proliferation of rationalizations seeking to explain the election results, the *New York Times* candidly viewed the vote as the product of extreme anti-war feeling.[39] Similar results were duplicated in other major cities.[40]

One of the primary objectives of the AALD was to increase productivity by inspiring the workingman to exert his utmost efforts and energies as a patriotic gesture in support of the war effort. This coincided with the aims of government and management. The result was a harmonious working relationship among the three. However, despite AFL cooperation, employers continued to complain that productivity was abnormally low, due to an indifferent and almost commercial attitude on the part of their employees.[41] Some even lamented

36. Robert Maisel to Stokes, March 28, 1918, Stokes MSS.
37. *The Fur Worker* 6 October 1917): 7.
38. *The World,* October 7, 1917, Stokes MSS.
39. *New York Times,* November 7, 1917, 12. *The Coast Seamen's Journal,* November 21, 1917, agreed with newspaper reports that Mitchell's defeat was due to his unprincipled labeling as unpatriotic those who disagreed with the war.
40. *International Socialist Review* 18 (September 1917): 182. The editor writes of the situation in Dayton, Ohio, where, for the first time, Socialist candidates had a real possibility of electing a majority to the City Commission.
41. O. Mueller to G. H. Howard, May 17, 1918, CPI Files, 1-A7(1), National Archives; L. J. Monahan to C. H. Howard, July 15, 1918, CPI Files, 1-A7(1), National Archives; Proposal for Executive Order by President Creating Industrial Patriotism Board, 1918, CPI Files, 1-A7(2), National Archives.

the fact that their workers were not acting in conjunction with Gompers and the AFL.[42] It became obvious that the call to patriotism was not producing the desired results among the workers. Many workingmen saw increased production as a boon to employers but of little benefit to themselves. Accompanying this attitude was a general lapse in all AALD work. In seeking an explanation, Chester Wright, head of the Division of Labor Publications, came to the conclusion that "intolerable working conditions" were undermining the work of the Alliance and that any "attempt to proceed with loyalty work without an adjudication of industrial conditions would be a pure waste of time."[43]

A realistic observer of worker attitudes and public opinion, Gompers was not unaware of the lack of popular support for the war.[44] However, he sought to combat it by using the twin tools of propaganda and repression. If "educational" propaganda did not prove altogether successful, Gompers was not hesitant in applying coercive measures. Given secondary consideration and minimal emphasis as a means of improving working-class support for the war was the development of any program to drastically improve labor's working conditions. AALD propaganda minimized unfavorable working conditions and placed particular emphasis on the future, with the declared hope that when the battle was over "the task of readjusting social conditions on principles of universal rights and justice . . ." would be given primacy at the peace table.[45]

Gompers's test for patriotism was simple, direct, and unencumbered: ". . . one . . . who since the declaration of war has . . . supported . . . the Government in the vigorous prosecution of the war to a complete and decisive triumph should be regarded as loyal."[46] The determination of what was "vigorous" was left to the arbitrary discretion of the authors. Thus, included in the category of disloyalty were millions of Americans who disagreed with the

42. H. E. Harris to C. H. Howard, July 17, 1918, CPI Files, 1-A7(1), National Archives.
43. Cited by Mock and Larson, *Words That Won the War,* pp. 203-4.
44. Franklin H. Martin, *Digest of the Proceedings of the Council of National Defense During the War* (Washington, D.C.: United States Government Printing Office, 1934), pp. 147, 348; Gompers to Organized Labor, January 1, 1918, *Official Magazine—Teamsters* 15 (February 1918): 2-5.
45. Mock and Larson, *Words That Won the War,* p. 198.
46. Gompers to Ralph Easley, May 20, 1918, Gompers MSS.

Administration's war aims or who had the temerity to challenge Gompers's policies within the AFL. Obviously, such broad definitions could and were used for personal advantage.

When the IWW posed a threat to AFL membership, Gompers sought to undermine its effectiveness by utilizing government agencies to help retard its growth. Bill Haywood claims that he was told by the writer Robert Bruere that Gompers was responsible for interesting the Department of Justice in its campaign to annihilate the IWW.[47] Government policy on deportations opened up the possibility of crushing radical labor organizations through wholesale arrests and expulsions.[48] The new Sabotage Act, under which the Department of Justice announced it would vigorously prosecute any person who interfered with the production of war goods, was recognized by labor men as intending "to drive large numbers of men who . . . had a casual acquaintance with . . . [the IWW] to form labor unions under the A. F. of L."[49] IWW papers and documents seized by the Justice Department were turned over to Gompers to help the Federation in its struggle with the radical Wobblies.[50] The AALD never protested against government incursions on free speech, right of assembly, or any of the questionable methods used to suppress the IWW. Quite to the contrary, it continued to fan the flames of hysteria by denying that the IWW served any labor function and labeling the organization as an agent of the Kaiser.

Once the AFL and the Alliance could define disloyalty, its orators sought to apply proper punishment for those it considered unfaithful to the nation. An example of its extremism can be seen in the statement of a Federation official who "asked that firing squads be called to deal with the Kaiser-branded seeker after peace. . . ."[51] The AFL, like Woodrow Wilson, tolerated no neutral position on the question of the war. "Each must stand up and be counted," the leadership intoned, "for those who are not with us [AFL] are against

---

47. William D. Haywood, *Bill Haywood's Book* (New York: International Publishers Company, 1929), p. 299.
48. Zechariah Chafee, Jr., *Free Speech in the United States* (Cambridge, Mass.: Harvard University Press, 1941), p. 227.
49. *Seamen's Journal* (May 8, 1918).
50. T. W. Gregory to Gompers, December 7, 1917, Department of Justice Files, Gregory Papers, National Archives, Washington, D.C.
51. *New York Times*, February 11, 1918, p. 1.

us."[52] Differences of opinion were smothered by stigmatizing the dissenters as traitorous.[53] Socialists like Adolf Germer, Victor Berger, and Morris Hillquit were branded by Gompers as German sympathizers, not only because of their views, but because of their ethnic German background.[54]

Gompers carried his campaign for loyalty into the shops. Dissent from established policies could often subject a worker to loss of his job. Niceties such as constitutional procedures were often ignored. The burden of proof was placed on the accused and he had to establish his innocence. Gompers seriously took under consideration arbitrary charges that groups of workers might be disloyal. A letter from the Trades and Labor Assembly in Minnesota stating that jobs held by German aliens who favored Germany should be filled by loyal Americans, and that a list of names of such persons was being compiled, was sent immediately by Gompers to Secretary of Labor Wilson for action.[55] It made no difference to Gompers that the list drawn up was based on subjective opinions and not overt acts.

Frightened by growing opposition to the war, Gompers supported all legislation rushed through Congress dealing with espionage and sedition. He was not overly concerned with setting up guidelines for freedom of speech and press. He was content to leave it to the government to determine what were the permissible boundaries.[56] Using such guidelines, the postmaster general felt justified in suppressing the *Nation* for either criticizing the methods used in apprehending draft dodgers or, as Chafee writes, more probably for criticizing Samuel Gompers.[57]

In order to ferret out "subversives" in the labor movement, Gompers worked closely with the Justice Department, going so far as to place labor men on the Department of Justice payroll to act as agents and informers. Ralph Easley of the NCF was usually his intermediary in such matters.[58]

52. *American Federationist* 25 (March 1918): 213.
53. *New York Times,* January 2, 1918, p. 7.
54. Speech at public meeting in Italy, October 8, 1918, in Gompers, *American Labor and the War,* pp. 262-63.
55. Gompers to William B. Wilson, February 18, 1918, Gompers MSS.
56. AFL, *Proceedings* (1917), pp. 92-93; *American Federationist* 25 (January 1918): 29-39.
57. Chafee, Jr., *Free Speech,* pp. 98-99.
58. Ralph Easley to Joseph P. Tumulty, May 5, 1917, NCF MSS; Thomas W. Gregory to Ralph Easley, April 2, 1918, NCF MSS.

If the original intention of the AALD was to serve as a propaganda instrument directed toward America's workers, it was soon to expand its functions by acting as an agent of the government in foreign countries. Its main area of endeavor was to be Latin America, particularly Mexico. Since the CPI was in close touch with the intelligence branches of the army and navy, the Alliance, in all probability, engaged in functions for Military Intelligence.

Organized labor in the United States had not reluctantly entered the field of international politics, but, instead, had initiated the idea and strongly urged the government to accept its services.[59] Gompers, upon his own initiative and later with the approval of President Wilson, opened up channels of communication with the labor movement of Japan for the express purpose of serving United States policy in the area.[60] In line with their desire to serve, Federation officials made several trips to Europe in an effort to induce European labor to support Allied war aims. Expenses for these trips were not borne by the AFL, but were wholly financed by agencies of the federal government.[61] This certainly opens up to question the possibility of the AFL's adopting an independent position in the realm of foreign affairs.

The craving of the AFL to be allowed to play a greater role in foreign-policy matters became ever more apparent in its ventures in Mexico, where it virtually implored the president to sanction its plans for the area.[62] In this endeavor, Gompers was not to be disappointed.

Gompers had sent an American Labor Mission to Mexico to report on the inroads made by German propaganda, and to suggest ways of educating the public to the United States viewpoint. The mission, convinced that German propaganda was finding a receptive ear in

---

59. W. A. Appleton to John P. Frey, July 24, 1918, Frey MSS. The letter was written by the secretary of the General Federation of Trade Unions who states that in agreement with Frey he found great acceptance in the British government for a closer association of labor with international politics.
60. Gompers to Woodrow Wilson, February 18, 1917, Wilson MSS: Gompers to Bunji Suzuki, February 18, 1917, Wilson MSS; Woodrow Wilson to Gompers, February 27, 1917, Wilson MSS.
61. Gompers to Executive Council, Confidential, August 14, 1918, Gompers MSS.
62. Gompers to Woodrow Wilson, April 16, 1918, Wilson MSS; Gompers to Joseph P. Tumulty, April 24, 1918, Gompers MSS.

Mexico, made several important suggestions: it formulated a plan for propagandizing the Mexican people; it recommended that the best agency to improve relations between the two governments was the organized labor movement of both countries; and, if the AFL was to conduct such a campaign, it advised that the government would have to bear the entire financial burden because labor was unable to do so.[63] Since Congress had cut appropriations for the CPI, Gompers suggested to President Wilson that the entire project be funded through the special fund placed by Congress at the disposal of the president for special wartime needs.[64] He recommended the money be placed in the hands of trustees, and that its disbursement be directed by the Executive Council of the AFL.[65]

In arguing for his proposals, Gompers further emphasized his belief that in foreign affairs organized labor had a "genuine function that [could] be served by no other agency."[66] That function, according to Gompers, could best be evaluated by answering the following question: "Can organized labor make friends for the United States where other agencies have failed?" Responding affirmatively, he pleaded with the president "that labor ought to be given the opportunity to accomplish this big thing in international relations. . . ."[67]

Wilson succumbed to Gompers's appeal, but differed with the federation chief on how to handle disbursements. After discussing the situation with Creel, Wilson decided to have the funds pass through the CPI in the same manner "as we have been using the Y.M.C.A."[68] The AALD was chosen as the instrument to carry on this work and funds were to pass through the hands of its treasurer, J. G. Phelps Stokes.[69]

The result was the establishment of a Pan-American Labor Press under the direction of James Lord, Santiago Iglesias, and John Murray. A limited number of issues were distributed in Mexico and the

63. Gompers to Woodrow Wilson, July 19, 1918, Gompers MSS.
64. *Ibid.*
65. Gompers to Woodrow Wilson, July 30, 1918, Gompers MSS.
66. *Ibid.*
67. *Ibid.*
68. Woodrow Wilson to George Creel, August 2, 1918, George Creel Manuscripts, Manuscript Division, Library of Congress, Washington, D.C.
69. Gompers to J. G. Phelps Stokes, August 8, 1918, Stokes MSS; Gompers to George Creel, August 8, 1918, Gompers MSS.

United States. Speaking tours and mass meetings were planned all the way from New York to Los Angeles, and along the border. The efforts of the Alliance appeared successful in checking German propaganda, and in bringing about the conference in Laredo, Texas, in November 1918, of the Pan-American Federation of Labor.[70] Thus, the AFL was to achieve its dual objectives: extension of its influence below the border and its development as an instrument in carrying out America's foreign policies. This was another example of one of those joint projects in which organized labor and the Wilson Administration cooperated in order to serve their mutual needs.

70. John Murray to Chester M. Wright, September 21, 1918, Stokes MSS; Leaflet, "Pan-American Labor's Mass Meeting," October 20, 1918, Stokes MSS.

10

Conclusion

The role of American labor in United States foreign policy has been a topic sorely neglected by scholars. Labor historians and economists have concentrated their efforts on detailing the history of the labor movement, the impact of collective bargaining on the economy, and the influence of organized labor on domestic politics, but until recently, few articles and certainly no books have appeared on the subject of labor and foreign policy. Yet, with the advent of the First World War and the beginning of America's expanded commitments abroad, organized labor has become an increasingly important factor in the carrying out of United States foreign policy. As labor's role has become more open and controversial, scholars have become concerned with the American Federation of Labor and its outlook on international affairs.

The international policies pursued by the AFL, and its successor, the AFL-CIO, were originally fashioned by Gompers in his reaction to the European conflict of 1914. Theoretically and structurally, the guidelines laid down by Gompers have found genuine sympathy and acceptance by his successors, William Green and George Meany. All that has changed is the context within which these policies are being carried out. Thus, an understanding of organized labor's role in the post-World War II era can best be grasped by means of an acquaintance with the fundamental principles that motivated Samuel Gompers to favor policies leading to a continuation and spread of the First

World War, and to hamper any negotiated settlement of the conflict on terms other than a "dictated peace."

Since this study purports to examine the impact of the AFL on this nation's foreign policy between 1914-18, an attempt will be made, at this point, to measure the degree of influence wielded by labor and to analyze the causes that propelled the AFL in the direction it was to follow. The result of this study indicates that the effect of organized labor on Wilson's foreign policies may be termed considerable. However, in order further to enhance our understanding of the role of the AFL in international affairs, it is necessary to examine in a more precise fashion, how, where, and on whom this influence was exerted.

At no time during the four years of the European War did the American workingman express any enthusiasm over the aims and objectives of the conflict. He was not apathetic to the war and United States involvement; he was hostile to it. However, the degree of hostility varied, and was especially pronounced prior to January 1918, when Wilson presented his ideas of the postwar settlement before a joint session of Congress. This attitude stimulated the forces of movement for peace, which became strong and articulate, and presented the main domestic threat to the Administration's policies overseas. It was within such a context that the leaders of the AFL were forced to operate in support of Wilson's program.

In that sector of the American population which had taken an active part in opposition to the war, the Federation was in a strategic and enviable position. Years of struggle against industry and government had given many of its leaders a degree of credibility with this group. The AFL was the largest institutional body and the most highly organized of all those groups engaged in reforming our economic system, and it, alone, was capable of giving mass impetus to the demands of many of its members for peace. Had the AFL mounted an offensive against the government's policies, it is more than likely that Wilson would have been forced to make drastic revisions in his policy of "reasonable preparedness," and in his decision to ask for a declaration of war against Germany. As a supporter of the president, the Federation was able to divide these forces of movement, deprive them of working-class support, narrow their base of support to a few ethnic groups and middle-class intellectuals, and, by this process of isolation, to make these groups susceptible to charges of disloyalty and anti-patriotism. More than any other man, Gompers was responsible for preventing the peace forces from drastically altering the foreign policies pursued by the Administration in Washington. If the labor movements in Europe were the largest single force pressing their respective governments in behalf of a peaceful termination of the conflict, in the United States organized labor was the most dependable supporter of the president in the struggle against a negotiated peace.

In addition to its role within the general framework of the anti-war movement, the AFL occupied a strategic position as an economic organization. Although it represented only a small fraction of the work force, its membership, composed largely of skilled craftsmen, was an indispensable factor in the production of war material. The success of Wilson's foreign policies, which rested to a great extent on a successful economic program at home, would largely be determined by the attitude of the rank and file of the AFL.

The membership of organized labor had a number of options open before it: 1) it could have refused to offer its wholehearted cooperation to the Wilson Administration because of an ideological antipathy to United States involvement in the war; 2) it could have adopted a purely trade-union position of seeking to gain at the bargaining table conditions it was not able to obtain prior to the war years; or conversely, 3) it could ideologically have supported Wilson's foreign policies and sought to ensure their success by minimizing its own economic demands so as to ensure tranquility at home by creating a harmonious working relationship between labor and management.

If the alternatives open to the workingman were considered within the context of worldwide labor unrest over the war and economic conditions at home, the concern of the Wilson Administration becomes apparent. Had the AFL supported either option 1 or 2, the consequences at home and abroad would have been catastrophic. *The New York Times* did not seek to minimize the importance of the cooperation of organized labor. A long-time antagonist of the AFL, the paper admitted in an editorial that had the AFL supported the peace movement or adopted a rigid attitude at the bargaining table, "there would have been strikes innumerable. Munitions, materials, and supplies of war could not have been had. There would have been an economic civil war, perhaps disorders and disturbances amounting to physical civil war. . . . The military and the moral effect would have been ruinous."[1]

Thus, the chief role of the Federation was twofold: to make the Government's foreign policies acceptable to America's workers, and to utilize its organization, not as a class weapon to extract maximum gains from the employer, but as an instrument to support national objectives. It was a classic case of the intertwining of domestic and foreign policy. The economic posture of the AFL was fashioned along lines that would support Wilson's policies abroad. If a clash developed between the class interest of the workers and the national objectives of President Wilson, then the former had to give way to the latter. To Gompers and the AFL hierarchy, the interests of the workingman were synonomous with the foreign-policy aims of the Wilson Administration.

Very little evidence could be found to sustain the thesis that organized labor played any substantial role in the actual creation of overall policy. Rather, it was content to react to policy once it had been formed. At no time during the European War did Gompers take a position on foreign policy that was in opposition to or contrary to the wishes of President Wilson. However, as the war continued, the AFL occasionally took a stand that was more militant than that which the Administration was advocating at the time.

In conclusion, the AFL acted primarily upon the public opinion of certain segments of the American people, but, as it became more deeply involved in foreign affairs, its position had to be taken into account by the president and the Congress. It was of immeasurable help in strengthening those forces within the government which took an uncompromising stand in their attitude toward Germany.

---

1. *New York Times,* September 4, 1917. The extent of worker dissatisfaction with the war and the crucial role of organized labor in war production is amply testified to by Secretary of Labor William B. Wilson in a speech in honor of George Creel, November 29, 1918, Department of Labor files, 16/446, National Archives.

At first blush, a comparison of the Federation's domestic and foreign policies appears so contradictory as to defy understanding. Since its inception, the AFL had waged a relentless struggle to increase its membership, to improve the lot of the skilled workers, and mainly to survive. It was at continual odds with the leaders of industry and government. Its domestic program was bitterly attacked by the National Association of Manufacturers as well as by presidents of the United States. Yet, as the United States began to entertain the idea of assuming the role of a world power, the AFL found itself in unaccustomed agreement with some of its lifelong opponents over the nation's policies abroad. This was partly due to the benevolent attitude toward organized labor adopted by the Wilson Administration. But in the main, it flowed from the theoretical conceptions of the AFL leadership regarding the role of organized labor in American society.

Although the preamble to the AFL Constitution reads like a Marxian call for the class struggle, the leaders of the Federation never envisioned such a role for labor. They were in complete agreement with the economic system and political institutions within which they lived and worked, and sought to bolster each. What the AFL desired, essentially, was to secure a place for itself within the established order. Its main problem lay in the fact that the major industrialists of the country regarded the trade unions as composed of trouble-making radicals, and the AFL as an institution detrimental to business. As a result, they were not willing to reach any accommodation whatsoever with the conservative trade-union leaders, and lost no opportunity in taking advantage of any situation to crush the labor movement.

Continuing employer hostility, which limited the growth of the craft unions, forced the AFL leadership to choose between two pressing alternatives: either to mobilize the working class and engage in mass struggles for workers' rights; or, conversely, to try to arrive at some agreement with employers by convincing the latter that trade unions, far from being a liability to business, could aid in increasing productivity and, furthermore, act as a preventive to the rise of more radical elements among the workers.

The former alternative offered some frightening possibilities. Once the workers were set in motion, the leaders of the Federation realized, they would be hard to stop and the end would be difficult to imagine. The momentum of such a movement might even carry it to the point where it would topple the conservative AFL leaders from their relatively secure positions of authority. Besides, the leaders of the Federation had little confidence in their ability to successfully organize mass numbers of workers and force the leading industrialists to engage in collective bargaining. With the decision of the AFL at the beginning of the twentieth century to participate in the work of the National Civic Federation, organized labor made known its decision to choose the latter alternative.

How to convince business of the identity of interest between it and labor became the chief preoccupation of the Federation. On the domestic front, labor found it difficult to convince industry of its "reasonableness." Any attempt by the Federation to soften its demands on "bread and butter" issues became immediately noticeable to the membership, and often evoked a high level of discontent and active opposition. Also, many of the officials of the national and international unions were vehemently opposed to such an approach and refused to cooperate in its implementation.

The election of Woodrow Wilson and the growing importance of international affairs in American life presented to Gompers and his allies a unique opportunity to implement their strategic concept of integrating the labor unions in the economic life of the nation by reaching a workable accord with the business community. Involvement in foreign affairs offered the leaders of the AFL certain distinct advantages. They could pursue a policy closely aligned to that of business and the government without evoking the same degree of antagonism that a similar position in domestic affairs would have induced. Of equal importance, they could easily camouflage their conservative position on foreign policy under a cloak of loyalty, patriotism, and true Americanism. Also, with the cooperation of industry and the Wilson Administration, Gompers foresaw an opportunity, in exchange for his pro-government stand, of utilizing both these groups to crush his enemies within the AFL and his opponents outside of it. Furthermore, Gompers viewed the expansion of United States influence abroad as being accompanied by a corresponding growth in

AFL prestige, thus enabling the Federation to play a leading role in the world trade-union movement. Acting under this premise, Gompers favored the granting of huge loans to the Allies because he felt it would lead to United States hegemony on the Continent and AFL dominance over the European trade unions. As the European War erupted, Gompers undertook as his primary task the unification of the American labor movement around the foreign policies of President Wilson.

The AFL became convinced that the war marked a turning point in the relations between industry and labor. It mistook the recognition granted it by the government and employers during the war as of a permanent nature and indicating the acceptance of labor as a necessary institution in the industrial sector. These hopes were to be cruelly smashed by the open-shop drive of the postwar era.[2]

A remarkable feature of the Federation's wartime program was its failure to anticipate the possibility that, once the emergency was over, the occupant of the White House or the leaders of industry might once again become hostile to the aims and objectives of the labor movement. Proclaiming that "labor is practical," the AFL belittled those "theorizing persons" who dared challenge the hope that a new world order would bring industrial democracy in its wake. To the AFL leadership, this meant keeping its feet upon solid, pragmatic ground.[3]

The charge has often been made that labor's support of a militant and aggressive foreign policy was due to its recognition that the economic consequences of such a policy—increased armament production and an expanding economy—would result in a decrease in unemployment, an increase in the average worker's pay envelope, and a rapid growth in union membership. Gompers would later support such a contention and claim that the AFL never entered into the anti-munitions campaign because it had greatly benefited from the manufacture of war supplies.[4] However, it is questionable whether,

2. William Green, *Labor and Democracy* (Princeton: Princeton University Press, 1939), pp. 68-95. Green, successor to Gompers as president of the AFL, provides a good description of labor's policies, hopes, and aspirations during the war period.
3. *American Federationist* 25 (October 1918): 915-16.
4. *New York Times,* May 3, 1917, p. 24.

in its early determination of policy, the AFL leadership perceived such a cause-and-effect relationship and was guided by it.

While Gompers's statement had elements of truth, the evidence does not support the degree of importance he attached to it. The compelling factor that led the Federation to favor President Wilson's policies on neutrality and preparedness was not economic, but part of an overall plan to align the Federation on the side of the government and the large Eastern banking and industrial interests for the express purpose of gaining for the AFL objectives it had long sought but had never been able to achieve: recognition and acceptance as a valid partner in the American industrial system. In other words, labor's foreign policy evolved primarily out of the theoretical conceptions held by the AFL as to its ability to survive and expand in a capitalist society and not as a direct result of immediate economic gain for its membership. It was only after the effects of Allied war orders and American rearmament became apparent that the Federation used the prosperity issue to pressure workers and union officials to follow its leadership. However, once the benefits of a revived economy began to be felt, the moral indignation of many of those opposed to rearmament and war began to give way to the practical gains derived from a foreign policy necessitating a wartime economy. It marked the beginning of organized labor's ties to the industrial and military sectors. This it saw as economically advantageous to the country as well as to its own future.

Although worker unrest remained high throughout the four years of war, the intensity of dissatisfaction began to abate after the publication of Wilson's "Fourteen Points" in January 1918. By imbuing the war with democratic aims and objectives, the president was able to ideologically undercut those in labor who were proponents of the idea that the war was being fought for capitalist gain. Coupled with the introduction of a War Labor Board that decided most issues in favor of labor, the anti-war forces in the labor movement began to experience a sharp decline. Gompers and Wilson, by persuasion and coercion, had been able to hold the lines of labor intact during the entire war period.

The results of Gompers's policies were to prove catastrophic for the labor movement. As soon as the emergency ended, labor lost its preferred status. The government was no longer anxious to please the labor leaders. Industrialists were determined to destroy whatever gains labor had made during the war. Because of its failure to extend unionism to the nonunion strongholds, and to insist on the closed shop in arrangements with the government, the AFL was unable to resist the coming onslaught.

Undeviating support of United States foreign policy was not to bring to labor the recognition it had so ardently sought. Armament production and a wartime economy were not the answers to labor's future. Yet, the labor movement still seems wedded to the same policies that caused it so much grief during the First World War.

Bibliography

Articles

"American Labor for No Half-Peace." *Literary Digest* (June 22, 1918), pp. 13-14.

Barnett, George E. "Dominance of the National Union in American Labor Organization." *Quarterly Journal of Economics* 27 (May 1913): 455-81.

Bourne, Randolph. "A Moral Equivalent for Universal Military Service." *New Republic* 7 (July 1, 1916): 217-19.

Carlton, Frank T. "Political Weakness of American Labor Organizations." *The Survey* (March 25, 1916), pp. 759-60.

————. "The Changing AFL." *The Survey* (November 21, 1914).

Davis, Malcolm W. "Labor and the Call to Arms." *New Republic* (June 10, 1916), pp. 137-39.

Dewey, John. "Universal Service as Education." *New Republic* 6 (April 22, 1916), 309-310.

————. "American Education and Culture." *New Republic* 7 (July 1, 1916): 215-17.

Fitch, John A. "Organized Labor in War-Time." *The Survey* (December 1, 1917), pp. 232-35.

————. "British Labor Out of It." *The Survey* (June 29, 1918), pp. 363-65.

"The Government and Organized Labor." *New Republic* 11 (July 7, 1917): 263-265.

Grubbs, Frank L., Jr. "Council and Alliance Labor Propaganda: 1917-1919." *Labor History* 7 (Spring 1966): 156-72.

162

Hendrick, Burton J. "The Leadership of Samuel Gompers." *The World's Work* 35 (February 1918).

Levine, Louis. "Federated Labor and Compromise." *New Republic* 1 (December 5, 1914): 14-15.

————. "Development of Syndicalism in America." *Political Science Quarterly* (September 1914), pp. 451-79.

Maddox, William P. "Labor's Stake in American Foreign Relations." *Political Science Quarterly* (September 1935), pp. 405-18.

Merz, Charles. "Labor in Convention." *New Republic* (November 24, 1917), pp. 90-92.

"Sam Gompers: Misleader of Labor." *The American Mercury* (October 1934), pp. 185-92.

Stelzle, Charles. "Labor in Council." *The Outlook* 108 (December 2, 1914): 761-62.

"Two Conventions at St. Louis." *The Independent* (December 15, 1910), pp. 1309-11.

Wehle, Louis B. "Labor Problems in the U. S. During the War." *Quarterly Journal of Economics* 32 (February 1918): 333-84.

West, George P. "The Progress of American Labor." *The Nation* 106 (June 29, 1918): 753.

————. "Labor Unpreparedness." *New Republic* (March 10, 1917), pp. 157-158.

Books

Addams, Jane. *Peace and Bread in Time of War*. New York: King's Crown Press, 1922.

Alinsky, Saul. *John L. Lewis*. New York: G. P. Putnam's Sons, 1949.

Babson, Roger W. *W. B. Wilson and the Department of Labor*. New York: Brentano's, 1919.

Baker, Ray Stannard. *Woodrow Wilson: Life and Letters*. 8 vols. Garden City, N. Y.: Doubleday, Doran and Co., 1939.

Baruch, Bernard. *American Industry In the War*. New York: Prentice-Hall, 1941.

Bell, H. C. F. *Woodrow Wilson and the People*. Garden City, N. Y.: Doubleday, Doran and Co., 1945.

Bimba, Anthony. *The History of the American Working Class*. New York: International Publishers, 1927.

Bing, Alexander M. *War Time Strikes and Their Adjustment.* New York: E. P. Dutton and Co., 1921.

Blum, John M. *Joe Tumulty and the Wilson Era.* Boston: Houghton Mifflin Co., 1951.

Carroll, Mollis Ray. *Labor and Politics.* Boston and New York: Houghton Mifflin Co., 1923.

Chafee Jr., Zechariah. *Free Speech in the United States.* Cambridge, Mass.: Harvard University Press, 1941.

Clarkson, Grosvenor B. *Industrial America in the World War.* Boston and New York: Houghton Mifflin Co., 1924.

Coit, Margaret L. *Mr. Baruch.* Boston: Houghton Mifflin Co., 1957.

Commons, John R. and Associates. *History of Labour in the United States.* 4 vols. New York: Macmillan Co., 1935.

Cronon, E. David, ed. *The Cabinet Diaries of Josephus Daniels.* Lincoln: University of Nebraska Press, 1963.

Curti, Merle. *Peace or War: The American Struggle, 1636-1936.* New York: W. W. Norton and Co., 1936.

Daniels, Josephus. *The Wilson Era.* 2 vols. Chapel Hill: University of North Carolina Press, 1944.

Dos Passos, John. *Mr. Wilson's War.* Garden City, N. Y.: Doubleday and Co., 1962.

Douglas, Paul H. *Real Wages in the United States, 1890-1926.* Boston and New York: Houghton Mifflin Co., 1930.

Filler, Louis. *Randolph Bourne.* Washington, D. C.: American Council on Public Affairs, 1943.

Fine, Nathan. *Labor and Farmer Parties in the United States.* New York: Russell and Russell, 1928.

Foster, William Z. *From Bryan to Stalin.* New York: International Publishers, 1937.

————. *Outline History of the World Trade Union Movement.* New York: International Publishers, 1956.

Ginger, Ray. *The Bending Cross.* New Brunswick, N.J.: Rutgers University Press, 1949.

Goldman, Eric F. *Rendezvous with Destiny.* New York: Alfred A. Knopf, 1952.

Gompers, Samuel. *Seventy Years of Life and Labor,* 2 vols. New York: E. P. Dutton and Co., 1925.

————. *American Labor and the War.* New York: George H. Doran Co., 1919.

————. *Labor and the Common Welfare.* New York: E. P. Dutton and Company, 1919.

Green, William. *Labor and Democracy.* Princeton: Princeton University Press, 1939.

Grubbs, Frank L. *The Struggle for Labor Loyalty: Gompers, the A.F. of L. and the Pacifists, 1917-1920:* Durham, N.C.: Duke University Press, 1968.

Gwynn, Stephen, ed. *The Letters and Friendships of Sir Cecil Spring Rice.* 2 vols. Boston and New York: Houghton Mifflin Co., 1929.

Hagedorn, Hermann. *Leonard Wood.* 2 vols. New York: Harper and Bros., 1931.

Haywood, William D. *Bill Haywood's Book.* New York: International Publishers, 1929.

Heaton, John L. *Cobb of "The World."* New York: E. P. Dutton and Co., 1924.

Hendrick, Burton J. *The Life and Letters of Walter H. Page.* 2 vols. Doubleday, Page & Co., 1922.

Hoover, Herbert. *The Ordeal of Woodrow Wilson.* New York: McGraw-Hill Book Co., 1958.

Hoxie, Robert Franklin. *Trade Unionism in the United States.* New York: D. Appleton & Co., 1923.

Josephson, Matthew. *Sidney Hillman: Statesman of American Labor.* Garden City, N. Y.: Doubleday & Co., 1952.

Karson, Marc. *American Labor Unions and Politics, 1900-1918.* Carbondale: Southern Illinois University Press, 1958.

Kellogg, Paul U., and Gleason, Arthur. *British Labor and the War.* New York: Boni and Liveright, 1919.

Lane, Anne Wintermute and Wall, Louise Herrick, eds. *The Letters of Franklin K. Lane.* Boston and New York: Houghton Mifflin Co., 1922.

Link, Arthur S. *American Epoch.* New York: Alfred A. Knopf, 1955.

————. *Wilson: The Struggle for Neutrality, 1914-1915.* Princeton, N. J.: Princeton University Press, 1960.

————. *Wilson; Confusions and Crises, 1915-1916.* Princeton, N. J.: Princeton University Press, 1964.

————. *Wilson: Campaigns for Progressivism and Peace, 1916-1917.* Princeton, N. J.: Princeton University Press, 1965.

Lombardi, John. *Labor's Voice in the Cabinet.* New York: Columbia University Press, 1942.

Lorwin, Lewis L. *The American Federation of Labor.* Washington, D. C.: Brookings Institution, 1933.

————. *Labor and Internationalism.* New York: Macmillan Co., 1929.

Madison, Charles A. *American Labor Leaders.* New York: Frederick Ungar Publishing Co., 1950.

Mandel, Bernard. *Samuel Gompers.* Yellow Springs, Ohio: Antioch Press, 1963.

Marot, Helen. *American Labor Unions.* New York: Henry Holt & Co., 1914.

Maurer, James Hudson. *It Can Be Done.* New York: The Rand School Press, 1938.

Mayer, Arno J. *Political Organs of the New Diplomacy, 1917-1918.* New Haven: Yale University Press, 1959.

————. *Politics and Diplomacy of Peacemaking, 1918-1919.* New York: Alfred A. Knopf, 1967.

Millis, Harry A., and Montgomery, Royal E. *Organized Labor.* New York: McGraw-Hill Book Co., 1945.

Millis, Walter. *Road to War.* Boston and New York: Houghton Mifflin Co., 1935.

Mock, James R., and Larson, Cedric. *Words That Won the War.* Princeton: Princeton University Press, 1939.

Morris, James O. *Conflict Within the AFL.* Ithaca, N. Y.: Cornell University Press, 1958.

Nevins, Allan. *Henry White, Thirty Years of American Diplomacy.* New York & London: Harper & Bros., 1930.

Norris, George W. *Fighting Liberal.* New York: The Macmillan Co., 1945.

Notter, Harley. *The Origins of the Foreign Policy of Woodrow Wilson.* Baltimore: The Johns Hopkins Press, 1937.

Palmer, Frederick. *Newton D. Baker.* 2 vols. New York: Dodd, Mead & Co., 1931.

Paxson, Frederick L. *America At War, 1917-1918.* Boston: Houghton Mifflin Co., 1939.

————. *Pre-War Years, 1913-1917.* Boston: Houghton Mifflin Co., 1936

Perlman, Selig. *A History of Trade Unionism in the United States.* New York: Macmillan Co., 1937.

Peterson, H. C., and Fite, Gilbert C. *Opponents of War, 1917-1918.* Madison, Wis.: University of Wisconsin Press, 1957.

Preston, Jr., William. *Aliens and Dissenters.* Cambridge, Mass.: Harvard University Press, 1963.

Pringle, Henry F. *The Life and Times of William Howard Taft.* 2 vols. New York: Farrar & Rinehart, Inc., 1939.

Raddock, Maxwell C. *Portrait of an American Labor Leader: William L. Hutcheson.* New York: American Institute of Social Science, Inc., 1955.

Reed, Louis S. *The Labor Philosophy of Samuel Gompers.* New York: E. P. Dutton and Co., 1919.

Saposs, David J. *Left Wing Unionism.* New York: International Publishers, 1926.

Seymour, Charles. *American Diplomacy During the World War.* Baltimore: The Johns Hopkins Press, 1934.

————. *The Intimate Papers of Colonel House.* 4 vols. Boston and New York: Houghton Mifflin Co., 1928.

Shaw, Albert, ed. *The Messages and Papers of Woodrow Wilson.* New York: Review of Reviews Corp., 1924.

Speranza, Florence Colgate, ed. *The Diary of Gino Speranza.* 2 vols. New York: Columbia University Press, 1941.

Taft, Philip. *The American Federation of Labor in the Time of Gompers.* New York: Harper and Bros., 1957.

————. *The A. F. of L. from the Death of Gompers to the Merger.* New York: Harper & Bros., 1959.

Thorne, Florence Calvert. *Samuel Gompers—American Statesman.* New York: Philosophical Library, 1957.

Trachtenberg, Alexander, ed. *The American Labor Year Book, 1917-1918.* New York: The Rand School of Social Science, 1919.

Van Der Slice, Austin. *International Labor, Diplomacy, and Peace, 1914-1919.* Philadelphia: University of Pennsylvania Press, 1941.

Viscount Grey of Fallodon, K. G. *Twenty Five Years.* 2 vols. New York: Frederick A. Stokes Co., 1925.

Von Rintelen, Captain Franz. *The Dark Invader.* New York: The Macmillan Co., 1933.

Walling, William English. *American Labor and American Democracy.* 2 vols. New York: Harper & Bros., 1926.

Walworth, Arthur. *Woodrow Wilson.* New York: Longmans, Green & Co., 1958.

Wehle, Louis B. *Hidden Threads of History.* New York: Macmillan Co., 1953.

Weintraub, Hyman. *Andrew Furuseth.* Berkeley and Los Angeles: University of California Press, 1959.

Wolman, Leo. *Ebb and Flow in Trade Unionism.* New York: National Bureau of Economic Research, 1936.

―――. *The Growth of American Trade Unions, 1880-1923.* New York: National Bureau of Economic Research, 1924.

Labor Publications

Amalgamated Clothing Workers of America. *Advance,* 1917-1918.

American Federation of Labor. *American Federationist,* 1914-1918.

―――. *History, Encyclopedia and Reference Book,* Vol. 1, 1919.

―――. *Report of Proceedings of the Annual Convention of the American Federation of Labor, 1914-1919.*

―――. *Weekly News Letter,* 1915-1918.

American Flint Glass Workers' Union of North America. *The American Flint,* 1914-1918.

Bakery and Confectionary Workers' International Union of America. *The Baker's Journal,* 1917-1918.

Boot and Shoe Workers' Union. *The Shoe Workers' Journal,* 1914-1918.

Bricklayers', Masons' and Plasterers' International Union of America. *The Bricklayer, Mason and Plasterer,* 1914-1918.

Brotherhood of Painters, Decorators and Paperhangers of America. *The Painter and Decorator,* 1914-1918.

Brotherhood of Railroad Trainmen. *The Railroad Trainman,* 1914-1918.

Brotherhood of Railway Carmen of America. *Railway Carmen's Journal,* 1914-1918.

Cigar Makers' International Union of America. *Cigar Makers' Official Journal,* 1914-1918.

International Association of Machinists, *Machinists' Monthly Journal,* 1914-1918.

International Brotherhood of Blacksmiths and Helpers. *The Blacksmiths' Journal,* 1914-1918.

International Brotherhood of Boilermakers, Iron Ship Builders and

Helpers of America. *The Boilermakers' Journal*, 1914-1918.
International Brotherhood of Bookbinders. *The International Bookbinder*, 1914-1918.
International Brotherhood of Electrical Workers. *The Journal of Electrical Workers and Operators*, 1914-1918.
International Brotherhood Teamsters, Chauffeurs, Stablemen and Helpers of America. *Official Magazine—International Brotherhood Teamsters, Chauffeurs, Stablemen and Helpers of America*, 1914-1918.
International Fur Workers' Union of the United States and Canada. *The Fur Worker*, 1914-1918.
International Ladies' Garment Workers' Union. *The Ladies' Garment Worker*, 1914-1918.
International Printing Pressmen and Assistants' Union of North America. *The American Pressman*, 1914-1918.
International Seamen's Union of America. *Coast Seamen's Journal*, later *The Seamen's Journal*, 1914-1918.
International Typographical Union of North America. *The Typographical Journal*, 1914-1918.
Journeymen Tailors' Union of America. *The Tailor*, 1915-1918.
Missouri State Federation of Labor. *The Labor Herald*, 1915-1918.
Pattern Makers' League of North America. *Pattern Makers' Journal*, 1914-1918.
United Brotherhood of Carpenters and Joiners of America. *The Carpenter*, 1914-1918.
United Mine Workers of America. *United Mine Workers' Journal*, 1914-1918.
United Textile Workers of America. *The Textile Worker*, 1914-1918.

Manuscripts

Newton Diehl Baker Papers, Manuscript Division, Library of Congress, Washington, D. C.
John Phillip Frey Papers, Manuscript Division, Library of Congress, Washington, D. C.
Samuel Gompers Papers, Manuscript Division, Library of Congress, Washington, D. C.
Robert Lansing Papers, Manuscript Division, Library of Congress, Washington, D. C.
National Civic Federation Papers, Manuscript Division, New York Public Library, New York City.

People's Council for Democracy and Peace, Tamiment Institute, New York.
James G. Phelps Stokes Papers, Butler Library, Columbia University, New York City.
Frank P. Walsh Papers, Manuscript Division, New York Public Library, New York City.
Woodrow Wilson Papers, Manuscript Division, Library of Congress, Washington, D. C.

Newspapers and Periodicals

International Socialist Review, 1914-1918.
The Masses, 1914-1915.
National Rip-Saw, later *Social Revolution*, later *Social Builder*, 1914-1918.
New York Call, October 7, 1917.
New York Times, 1912-1919.

United States Government Documents and Publications

Committee on Public Information Files, National Archives, Washington, D. C.
Department of Justice Files, National Archives, Washington, D. C.
Department of Labor Files, National Archives, Washington, D. C.
Martin, Franklin H. *Digest of the Proceedings of the Council of National Defense During the War*. Washington, D. C.: U. S. Government Printing Office, 1934.
U. S. Committee on Industrial Relations. *Final Report and Testimony*. Vol. 2. Washington, D. C.: U. S. Government Printing Office, 1916.

Unpublished Material

Grubbs, Frank Leslie. "The Struggle for the Mind of American Labor." Ph.D. dissertation, University of Virginia, 1963.
Jones, Dallas Lee. "The Wilson Administration and Organized Labor." Ph.D. dissertation, Cornell University, 1954.
McKee, Delber Lee. "The American Federation of Labor and American Foreign Policy, 1886-1912." Ph.D. dissertation, Stanford University, 1952.

Index

171

Date Due			